MY GOOD
PORTSMOUTH

Michael Franckeiss

ARTHUR H. STOCKWELL LTD.
Elms Court   Ilfracombe   Devon
Established 1898

British Library Cataloguing-in-Publication Data.
A catalogue record for this book is available
from the British Library.

By the same author:
I Never Cried
Grandad's Air Force

Cover photo: The Guildford Street gang — 1937–38
Yours truly second from left, aged about four years

ISBN 0 7223 3374-9
Printed in Great Britain by
Arthur H. Stockwell Ltd.
Elms Court   Ilfracombe
Devon

CONTENTS

ACKNOWLEDGEMENTS

To my dear parents and others who did their very best for me through difficult times. To my dear wife for putting up with me for so long and my children and grandchildren of whom I am very proud. Not to forget my son David for turning my long hand into legible print. As this is a story of a working man, I think it would be very appropriate to offer a big thank you to all of my very loyal customers for their support over a long period of time.

INTRODUCTION

I realise, of course, how very presumptuous it is of me to even imagine that people would want to read my life story. Many thousands of people have led a far more interesting life than I have that has never been recorded, and very often important events in a family's history are lost forever. What you will read is an honest and factual account of my life in Portsmouth; some not so good, but many more that were good. This has not been an attempt by me to write a novel; I will leave that to the real authors. It is purely and simply my memories of my childhood and adult life, with comments and opinions as I thought necessary to make my point. Believe me when I say that I make no claim, whatsoever, of being an academic or a literary expert. What I ask you to do, dear reader, is to forgive, or overlook the grammatical mistakes that will appear quite often in this narrative. A combination of a very limited education and, I must admit, my lack of enthusiasm in the subject, and added to the mix, a world war, are my main excuses for my little, or no, expertise. However, if I am able to leave an account of my life for future generations of the Franckeiss family to read and, hopefully, take an interest in, then that is all I ask. May I give to you, dear reader, my heartfelt thanks for taking time to read this account of a very 'ordinary' person's life.

VERY EARLY BEGINNINGS

The Franckeiss family have lived in and around the Portsmouth area for many years, and a Franckeiss has worked in the dockyard at Portsmouth from 1851 to the present time. My surname is of French-German origin, and the name came to these shores in 1240. Church records on the Isle of Wight show many Franckeiss families living there, and the earliest record that I have seen is 1580. As you would have realised I am very interested in genealogy, and I spend many hours in the very fine search room of the Portsmouth Museum, learning of my family's past life.

In 1851, two shipwrights are recorded. One lived in Cumberland Street, the other in York Street in Portsea. Also a tobacconist lived in Queen Street, Portsea, plus one who was a draper. An interesting Mrs Franckeiss ran a lodging house in Unicorn Street, and is listed as a straw bonnet maker; a very busy lady!

In 1715, Henry Franckeiss came across the water from Ryde to marry a Portsmouth lady by the name of Mary Dolman. I have very many records of my ancestors, but I will not take the risk of boring you. I fully realise that one person's interest is not necessarily the interest of others.

DIFFICULT TIMES

54 Manchester Road, Fratton. That is an address that would mean very little, if anything at all, to readers of this story. My parents rented the front room upstairs and the front room downstairs, with the use of the scullery (what an evocative word that is), and a trip outside to use the toilet. This accommodation was rented from Mrs Waterman who occupied the remainder of the house.

I was born in that house on the 16th of January 1933. I was the third child of the marriage, with brother John being the eldest, then next was my sister Kathleen. Therefore, in those two rooms lived the five of us.

It is difficult to imagine how my mother managed. I do know that at the time that I was born my father was unemployed. Not unusual for the time, as many people were looking for work. I did once meet the son of Mrs Waterman (my parents' landlady) just by sheer coincidence, and he was able to give me a good deal of first-hand knowledge about my mother and father at the time of my birth. I was very grateful to him. I think that it is a fact of life that children never seem to talk enough to their parents, and a lot of family history is lost forever. I plead guilty to this. It was only after my parents passed away, that I wished that I had spoken to them more often about their early married life, and many other questions regarding my family history. Managing in that little house, cooking, etc., would have, I am sure, taken a lot of organising for both families, and I am sure that they did it successfully. I understand that both families were on very good terms.

1934 saw my father's fortunes change regarding employment, as he was taken on as the manager of a wet fish shop in Queen Street, Portsea. If it were possible I would name the company, but I do not have the information; just a little example of not talking to parents!! My father, having found employment, was then able to look for better accommodation for the family. Mrs Waterman had let the two rooms to my parents for a very low rent, which, of course, proved a great help, but the cramped conditions at number 54 could not continue. A property to rent was found at 44 Cottage View in Landport (not to be confused with Cottage Grove in Southsea). The house that my parents were able to rent was not, by any stretch of the imagination, a luxury dwelling, but they now had the whole house to themselves, and it must have made my mother very happy.

I would like to spend a little time describing the layout of the house to you. The little house in Cottage View was identical to many houses in the older part of Portsmouth. The front door opened onto the pavement, with a short passage of about nine feet in length, leading to the room between the scullery and the front room. The size of the four rooms (two bedrooms, living room and front room), was nine feet by nine feet approximately, with the scullery being smaller. The back yard was about fifteen feet by ten feet, with the toilet standing at the bottom of the yard; a horrible place to visit at night!! One of the reasons being it was difficult to see the cut-up newspapers hanging on a nail on the wall, which the whole family used as toilet paper.

An old brick copper stood at one end of the scullery for boiling water. A shallow butler sink with a wooden draining board, was my mother's fitted kitchen! The house had a gas supply and this was to the New World gas cooker, and, of course, all the house had gas lighting. I often had to go on an errand to buy a one penny mantle from Timothy Whites. In my opinion they were more fragile than a bird's egg, and breaking it was a genuine fear. My parents owned a very large wooden roller mangle; I suppose at this time it was classed as a modern implement, and it did remove a lot of water from the washing. The scullery floor consisted of flagstones, and swilling out was the usual form of cleaning.

The staircase led up to the bedrooms from the living room, and access to the stairs was gained by opening a kind of cupboard door. I think that without this door one hell of a draught would have made sitting in the room intolerable. Open fires were the order of the day at this time. Although the four rooms all had fireplaces, the living room fireplace was the main one used. If there was sickness in the family in wintertime and it meant being confined to bed, then a fire would be burning in the grate upstairs.

The three kids, John, Kath and yours truly, were in the back bedroom, and I am pretty sure in saying that we were not allowed to have the gaslight on, but we did take a candle; maybe because it would have been cheaper than the gas.

With the kids out of the way, Mum and Dad were able to listen to the wireless, or the alternative would be listening to a few records on the wind-up gramophone. The gramophone was a rather decent piece of furniture; it stood on four nicely shaped legs, supporting a polished cabinet for storing records in. It had a turntable and a little area set aside for the brass needles. The singers' names that I recall are Al Boley, John McCormack, Donald Peers and 'The Singing Cowboy' Gene Autry, plus many others.

Payment for the gas was by a penny in the slot gas meter, and every so often the meter would be emptied. The gasman would appear at the end of the street, and in no time at all my mother had heard that he was about. A chair would be taken from the front room into the passage and placed ready for the gasman. Why these gas meters were installed in such awkward places, I shall never know. But that is not all, the air was always filled with expectancy, as all the housewives were hoping for a rebate. I have never known how the rebate system worked, but I feel sure that it could have been a nice little earner for the gasman. The cash box contents were emptied onto the chair, and a count up was the next stage, and at the end of a very anxious wait for my mother was, "There you are missus, a 1/4 rebate". It seems incredible that these few coppers would mean having enough money to buy groceries for the family for at least one day. My mother always offered the gasman a cup of tea; rebate or no rebate. By the time that he had cleared the meters in the street, he was loaded down with bags of copper coins, but where he off-loaded this money I have no idea. Rebates were always discussed by the neighbours; some had happy faces and some would appear a bit glum. Not surprising that those few pennies meant a lot to so many people!

Furniture was fairly sparse in our house; just enough for the family's needs. Although, in keeping with a lot of the houses at this time, our front room was a bit posher than the rest of the house. The odd visitor would be shown into the front room, but I always imagined that it was meant only for the insurance man. The insurance book with the money was always left on the chair just inside the door. Everybody in the street would have known this; mainly because it was the method used by most people to pay different callers, but never, in my memory, was money ever stolen. The front door key was hanging on a piece of string the other side of the letter box; anyone could have entered the house. This is an example of the faith and trust that people had in each other in Portsmouth in the 1930s.

Another pastime that my mother had, was mat making; not only a pastime but a necessity. These mats were made out of any old cloth, cut into strips and threaded through hessian. Old coats and blankets were the ideal material, but with a lot of people using the same discarded kind of material, it was difficult to come by. This kind of DIY mat would never be classed as elegant, but they made one hell of a difference to the cosiness and appearance of the passage and rooms.

My mother worked hard to make a home for her family with very little resources. Unfortunately it is not until we are grown up that we realise this, but I suppose that kids will always be the way they are, with stock questions like "What's for tea, Mum?" and "Can I have my pocket money, Dad?" My mother's main recreation was reading, but she only found time to read in the evenings as she was such a busy person. I have always felt that well organised women will always work a day or two in advance, and will do a tomorrow task today.

It was not until 1940, when the family were blitzed out of Cottage View and had moved to Milton Road, that I learned of my mother's well-kept secret that she could play the piano. She was unable to read music, but she could play all the pop tunes of the day. I always wondered how the family were able to afford a piano, and it was not until later that I learned that the piano had been left by the previous occupants of the house, who had moved out when a 'land mine' dropped out of the sky and landed at the bottom of Bowler Avenue; destroying the Airspeed Social Club and many houses. A strange thing to leave, but strange things happened in wartime Portsmouth.

My father allowed himself recreation by going fishing. This was a useful hobby of my father, as very often he would bring something home for the pot. A friend of his kept a boat down by The Hard; his friend being John Tout (Gus), and their fishing venue would normally be the upper reaches of the harbour. Very often a good chance of a flatfish or two could be had from that area. My father was very good at preparing fish and poultry; also rabbit for cooking.

I have always admired my parents for being so clever at so many different tasks. They always overcame problems and seemed to be able to use their brains to overcome many difficult situations that arose. Given a chance in life, with better education, I feel that my father would have earned his living in a professional way. Both my parents were from large families, and I think that this fact curtailed their progress; having to start work at such an early age. I am sure that many people of their era had the same difficult situation thrust upon them.

As this narrative is of memories, I would like to put on record what I think is my first memory in Portsmouth. I can remember the Fleet lying in The Solent in preparation for the review in 1937. I was with my parents on the promenade at the Clarence Parade end of Southsea seafront, and I was standing in a forest of legs. I can remember hearing a hubbub of voices; just people talking to each other. I certainly was not cold, so I think the weather was quite balmy. All the ships were dressed from stem to stern and with lights. My father had hoisted me onto his shoulders. That is my earliest memory, and it has been with me all of my life. I was born in 1933, so I will leave you to work out my age and the date of the Fleet review that I remember from the thirties!

FOOD

Whistle in the dark — I can recall three fish and chip shops very near to where I lived. Two were in Arundel Street and the third was in Railway View, and was run by the Cantwell family. Our family always preferred the latter; maybe it was the kind of fat which was used in the frying of the fish and chips. I always looked forward to our fish and chip nights; to me it was a kind of a treat. I know of no better meal eaten with home-made pickled onions and crusty bread and butter. A meal fit for any Pompey lad, with hot sweet tea to complete the treat. The time span is sixty years, and I still enjoy the good Olde English Fayre of fish and chips. We can forget about kebabs and curry — the sooner the better!

Very often it was my job to run to the shop to collect the supper. I was frightened of the dark, but even at that young age too proud to tell my parents. I did not mind so much if it was a moonlit night; one side of the street would be in shadow; the part that I avoided at all cost! When walking on the bright side, I always whistled, no tune of course, just whistle. If it was a moonless night, then I would run like the wind. I had no need to be frightened, because in the thirties there was no thought of five and six-year-olds being molested by perverts. I think the reason for whistling was to keep the evil spirits away!

Winkles for tea — I will continue to write about food and the way that we were fed in the thirties. In my opinion, it is a very important subject and well worth recording. Street vendors we had in abundance, and a regular Sunday morning cry could be heard of "Come and get your winkles, 2d. a pint".

Also cockles were on sale, but always a little bit dearer. All the same though, a very good buy. The man who hawked them around the streets, would be the man who had gathered them, purged and cleaned them, and had cooked them to perfection. Eaten with vinegar and a touch of pepper, they were a Sunday treat! Perhaps, on another Sunday, winkles would be on the menu for tea. Did I say menu? That was our tea — winkles — eaten with bread or margarine or sometimes butter. We had fun and competition, seeing who could extract the poor little creature from its shell in one piece with our pins; this was a bit of an art acquired with time. Nevertheless, a simple but tasty meal, and above all within budget.

An essential part of any family's diet would, of course, be fruit and vegetables. There were many vendors of these commodities, but a favourite in the area was Dick Kneller who also had premises on the corner of Netley Street. My mother always held Dick Kneller in high esteem. I know this because whenever she spoke of him in later years, she would always emphasise how very kind he was to the people in Cottage View. Money was usually very scarce, but Dick seemed to be prepared to wait for payment. He knew his customers, and I would not mind betting that there were never many defaulters. The children in the street would ask for any pecked fruit that he might have; sometimes they were unlucky, but it was always worth a try. I am sure that many of you remember the Knellers' fruit and veg, and the family still have shops operating in Portsmouth.

A hard lesson — A plus factor of living in an area such as Landport, was the availability of a wide range of shops all within easy walking distance. I am a great believer in small shops in local areas; they are a great builder of communities. Those shopkeepers always knew how to serve a customer, and invariably greeted you by name. Today's supermarkets bear no comparison to the corner shop of yesterday.

On one corner of Cottage View stood a bread and cake shop, and always freshly-baked produce could be had. The proprietor, I believe, was a Mr White who was a Salvation Army member; possibly with the rank of Captain. His bakery was directly opposite his shop, just across Arundel Street; hence his fresh bread and cakes. My mother would send me to his shop for a bag of yesterday's cakes. Yesterday or not, I would always scoff them! His baker was a very friendly man. I do know that he lived in Besant Road, and I would like to be able to name him for any relatives who might read this book; he was a kind and pleasant man. I would spend time in the bakery watching him at his work. I am very sure that the delightful smell of the baking of the bread and cakes was for me one of the main attractions; and the odd titbit I received from the baker. Temptation was to come my way in the form of a jam tart. Trays of these 'melt in the mouth' items were being taken from the oven and left to cool on the long work table in front of me. The baker, just for a moment, had moved out of sight, and for me the temptation had proved just too much. I stole one of the freshly-baked jam tarts! I shot out of the bakery with my ill-gotten prize. Once outside I could not resist taking a bite, but the hot jam punished me for being a sneak thief, and it burned the inside of my mouth. "Serves you right" I hear you all say, and how right you all are. I had returned the man's kindness by stealing his produce. The pain I suffered with my scolded mouth, will always remind me to think again when considering any future misdeeds. A hard lesson had been learned.

More street vendors — Another popular voice to be heard on a Sunday, would be that of the muffin man. Yet more goodies brought to your door and generally affordable. If it was the winter season then, of course, the muffins would be toasted by the coal fire. Is it only imagination, or is it a fact, that items toasted by an open fire always seemed to taste nicer than those toasted under a grill? — or am I just an oldie, just a little bit full of nostalgia? Two muffins each was the ration, unless a member of the family refused his or her share; I am bound to say a most unlikely event.

The toffee apple was another tasty item on offer from the street vendors. Most were of very good quality, but the less reputable vendors would try to palm you off with apples that were purchased cheaply, from the market in Charlotte Street late on Saturday, when the stallholder wished to reduce his stock. Apart from the apple itself, I liked to eat the thick dark treacle toffee, that formed a kind of platform by running over and setting on the bottom of the apple. My parents were not always able to afford these treats for us kids, and when they said you were unable to buy these items, it was no good trying to badger them into changing their minds. They said no and meant it! You had to accept the decision.

Verrechia and Dagostino were two of the main ice-cream vendors of the time, and of course, once again, it depended on how the family's finances were, whether you got an ice cream or not. It is a fact, that at this time in my life, that as little as an ice cream would have cost, it was not always possible for my parents to afford it.

Good quality meat — My mother shopped in Stevens the butcher for her meat. The shop was only a matter of yards away in Arundel Street. As I have said, who needs supermarkets? Stevens were probably one of the largest purveyors of meat in the area, and my mother had no need to look any further than Stevens for good quality meat. A meal that the family always enjoyed was bacon bone and lentil soup; eaten, of course, with chunks of bread. I use the word 'eaten' intentionally; although called soup, it was more of a solid meal; we always had second helpings. The bacon bones were inexpensive to buy, and this was really a super meal. Imagine buying at today's prices, six rolled and stuffed breasts of lamb for one shilling; and yet another inexpensive item. This was the basis for a really excellent meal, and as always, cooked to perfection; eaten with relish; not even the fat was allowed to stay on the plate!

Considering the fact that my mother was always catering for the family on a very strict and limited budget, the meals that she provided for the family were a real credit to her. She would put present-day so-called economists in the shade if it came to a management contest. Maybe all men say this about their mothers, but I say it with all sincerity.

Tuck shop scams — I liked to spend any pocket money that came my way on sweets. It was by no means certain that I would have had pocket money given to me on a regular basis, and this was probably the situation for the other children of that era regarding pocket money. I am prepared to say that the price of sweets at this time, and many other items, was a true reflection of the low wages that were had in the area in this period of time. Here are just a few examples of sweets that could be bought for a penny or under; small toffee bars, gobstoppers, sherbet dabs, liquorice shoelaces, bags of peanut brittle and chocolate mice; I always started eating my mouse head first! Please remember, dear reader, that in the thirties a penny, a halfpenny and a farthing had real purchasing power, unlike the penny of today's decimal currency.

One very nice corner shop stood on the corner of Guildford Street and Arundel Street, and the delightful lady who ran this gem was Miss Coles. Always a busy shop, it sold groceries, tinned food, bread, cakes, bread rolls, biscuits and very many other things that people in the neighbourhood wished to buy. Always available was cooked ham on the bone; a real favourite. This lovely piece of meat stood on the counter, and also on the counter sat a large black and white cat. Hygiene? What is that? The display and cleanliness of the shop was never at fault. Miss Coles herself wore a pristine wraparound apron; her hair nicely tied in a bun, and somehow always gave the impression of being clean; which, I am sure, she was. A good deal of her business owed a lot to the patronage of the girls who were employed in the corset factory that stood in Landport Street, which was bombed to the ground on a terrible night in World War Two, when so many people lost their lives. In her innocence, Miss Coles had her collection of sweets set out along the front of the counter; a fact not to be missed by us scallywags. We knew her busiest time of day of course, and that would be our time to strike. Not a nice thing to admit, but I did snatch some sweets when I knew the time was right. The chance of freebies ceased when the dear lady realized what was happening to her stock, and the fact that it was in a very vulnerable position, and removed the temptation from us little brats.

Yet another little sweetshop stood on the corner of Cottage View and Arundel Street. Two elderly ladies were the proprietors. Unfortunately I am unable to relate their names to you. On the wall of the shop, just inside the door, a penny in the slot machine was mounted. A penny placed into the slot would produce a Bakerlite counter, either red, green, blue or yellow, and these counters had varying degrees of value. Red being the most sought-after colour. If you were lucky enough to win the red one, then you would be entitled to threepenny worth of sweets of your choice; a real prize to be had. The red counters were, of course, very few and far between; so what is new? Just by coincidence at this time ludo counters were made of the same material as the counters from the machine, a bad oversight by the manufacturers, but something not unnoticed by the scallywags! I realise, dear reader, by now you are ahead of me and you are quite correct, we did attempt to swap the counters for a higher value, and for a time we

B

did succeed with the little scam, but when we were found out, we had the bollocking of our lives from these genteel ladies, and we were banned from the shop. Never mind, our alternative would be to walk along to Stevens, the home-made boiled sweetmakers, and we could buy a pennyworth of 'dusties' from the bottom of the jar. What have my grandchildren missed?

PEOPLE OF MY STREET

I remember a number of people who lived in Cottage View. I will name a few of them, and I would like to add some of the memories that I have of my neighbours of long ago.

The Phillips family lived on the Crasswell Street side of Cottage View, and were good friends of my parents; my mother always spoke of 'Dollie' as a genuine person.

Opposite our house lived the Russells. They lived in a house entirely different to any other property in Cottage View. It was a detached property that stood in its own grounds. It had a little front garden enclosed with a picket fence; a real novelty for the area! It was a very cottage-like building and, who knows, this building maybe the reason for the name Cottage View? I am open to contradiction on this one; I am not sure of my facts. Back to the people. Harry Russell's occupation was that of a milkman. Harry was always neatly dressed. I can picture him now in his ginger-coloured tweeds; jacket, waistcoat, trousers and brown leather highly-polished gaiters; also the obligatory collar and tie. Harry pushed his three-wheeled cart, which was nicely varnished and 'sign-written'. The milk was in a large brass churn and other small containers; not to forget, of course, the milk dipper. Mrs Russell, for some reason, always made me feel welcome in her house. I have always been puzzled by kindness towards me, as generally I was known as 'that little sod' by other people in the street. As they say, there is no accounting for taste. Harry Junior was always very kind to me; he was about twenty years of age, and the woman that he was about to marry was a fiery redhead. If I happened to be in the house when she arrived, a feeling of uneasiness would always come over me. I always felt that she resented me being in the house, and in subtle ways she let me know it. Mrs Russell always showed me great kindness, but I always made a hasty exit when the future daughter-in-law arrived! An elderly couple lived next door to us (No.42); a Mr and Mrs Hutchings. Joseph had a disability and walked with the aid of a stick. He was a retired man and when he was not tending his rabbits, which he bred mainly for the Christmas table, he would sit on the front room windowsill watching the world go by. Joe was also the street's moneylender; not I might add out of the kindness of his heart, but at a percentage. I think the agreed terms would be something like, borrow two shillings from him and pay two shillings and sixpence back. To be fair to Joe, he did take a bit of a risk lending money. People in the street were never too sure of their employment from one day to the next, so on the face of it, lending money at a percentage, was a reasonable thing to do. In those days, many children were allowed to play in the street which, in the main, was a very safe play area. Hardly any, or no traffic, and evil perverts were unheard of. Very often, on a Monday, Mrs Hutchings would appear at her front door; not to tell us to clear off, but to hand out cold baked spuds. I always had the feeling that these potatoes, heavily coated with congealed fat, were the leftovers from the previous day's lunch. I did make an attempt at eating one of Granny Hutchings' cold spuds. Believe me, dear reader, when I say that I just could not afford to be a fussy eater. The times would have never allowed a kid to be that choosy, but these greasy cold spuds would not stay down. They were used as ammunition aimed at kids from the next street and would hastily be gobbled up by the pigeons. On reflection I realise what callous little sods we were. Mrs Hutchings was attempting to do us a very good turn. Why did us kids not understand this? I understand now, of course. What I would give to be able to say "Thank you for the potatoes, Mrs Hutchings"!! If I had said that at the time, it would have pleased her greatly!

I feel sure that I am right in saying, that in any community, there will always be an oddball, and sure enough, Cottage View had been blessed with one such person. Her name was Mrs Ings and she was a misery guts. Us kids avoided the front of her house like the plague. You could liken her front door to a Venus flytrap. Be near it with your ball or whip and top, or even your marbles, and the door would spring open and she would take possession of them. It would take all sorts of arguments and rows between her and the parents before there was any chance of getting your property returned. She seemed to have a one-woman crusade against children playing in the street. I would think that she led a very lonely life. She was so unfriendly. The day came for her to move; a move that was to please everyone. She left a tea chest in the garden almost full with confiscated balls! I think everybody said good riddance to the old misery guts.

My parents were good friends with the Kings, Harry and ?, who lived at No.38. They were to die in very tragic circumstances. They had moved to Landport Street because of the bomb damage to their house in Cottage View. They were killed when their house was blitzed during one terrible air raid. Those dear people were never found. At this awful time, their two sons Harry and Bill, were serving in the Army. One can only imagine what their reaction would have been on receiving such news of their parents' deaths. What does war ever solve?

I could never write about the people of Cottage View, without writing about the Faithwaite family. There was Mrs Faithwaite, Flo, her husband Lance and the children, Gordon, Douglas, Roy and the lovely Marie. For some strange reason Flo took a liking to me, as did her children. The Faithwaite's home was to become my second home; I was treated as one of the family. I will never understand Flo liking me. Perhaps she liked ugly kids?

Lance, like many Portsmouth people, was employed in the dockyard. Flo would always have his tea cooked ready for when he returned from work. Somehow I always contrived to be in the house at this time, and for a very good reason. Flo always gave me a helping of whatever had been prepared for Lance, and what's more, Lance never seemed to mind me being there. Many a winter evening I have spent in Flo's cosy living room. As a special treat she would send me along to the Lamb and Flags' bottle and jug to buy one or two hot pies. They were called 'Ticky Snacks', and for a few pence we had a tasty treat. These pies were so good that the Royal Marines' Sergeants' Mess caterer would cycle all the way from Eastney Barracks to buy these tasty pies. I was told this interesting fact in later years by Mac the landlord.

Another bright spot in my life, was being taken by Flo to pick strawberries. I am not sure what means of transport we used, probably a coach; or should I say charabanc? Yet another precious memory.

One day, whilst in Flo's company, I used a couple of bad words, as some children at times do out of sheer bravado. Flo pretended to be angry at me saying "Uncle Lance will be angry at you when he comes home. I will tell him about you using those naughty words and he will not give you any of his tea." I was willing to take that chance. I heard him coming and I hid under the table. I was not frightened of Lance, far from it, but I was guilty of swearing. The game went on and Lance had been given the nod. "Where is that Mickey tonight, then Flo? I think that this tea I am eating is his favourite. It looks as though I will have to eat it all myself." I could stand it no longer. "I am under here, Uncle Lance. I didn't mean to swear." There we are folks, the first under-the-table confessional was in Cottage View. "Come on, sit up in your chair and hold your plate out" he said. Who needs money when you have memories such as these?

The two eldest Faithwaite boys, Gordon and Doug, were keen boxers and they belonged to the St Faiths' Youth Club in Crasswell Street. I know that they were good at their sport as they had many trophies, cups, etc., on show in the front room of their house in Cottage View. Gordon made a career in the Army as a Physical Training Instructor, and Flo was very proud of the fact that her son appeared on television as a boxing referee in the Inter Services' Boxing Competition. Marie was also a member of St Faiths and took part in the stage shows which were open to the public. I was taken by Flo to see one of their productions. I can remember Marie taking part, and she sang and danced to the tune of 'I'm Going To Lock My Heart And Throw Away The Key'. How do I remember that particular part of my life? Don't ask!

Roy was a friendly and unassuming man, and his sport was football. In the late forties/early fifties, he was Secretary of Arundel Street Sports; one of the first Sunday League sides. He also played for them as centre half, and had the grand nickname of Cocoa. They held their club meetings in a room of the Spread Eagle in Arundel Street, by kind permission of Edna the landlady. Edna and Auntie ran the Spread Eagle, and were very popular in the area. I believe that Flo washed the team's kit every week; washed and dried ready for the next game. I wonder if the team of old know this?

Dearest Florence lived for a long time and became ill. I often visited her but towards the end, her illness prevented her from knowing who I was and that hurt me so much. I know that I am a much better person for having the good fortune of being a friend of that wonderful lady. I sincerely regret not being aware of her death, and therefore being unable to pay my last respects at her funeral, so maybe what I have written will somehow make amends.

A TERRIBLE EVENT

Quite possibly my age would have been about three or four, so I am not fully aware of the facts, but I will tell the story as I know it. It was an event that was to affect my whole family.

My eldest brother, John, who was seven years old at the time, was struck by a vehicle whilst walking along Arundel Street. It may have been a car, but it was more likely a motorcycle that caused this hit and run. The evil person who injured my brother so severely, never even had the guts or moral fibre to come forward and was never found. My brother lived in spite of his terrible injuries, in which one of his legs was shattered and this meant the loss of a kneecap, plus many other injuries.

My father has since told me that he was amazing during the operations and treatment of his shattered limbs. He had major surgery and on-going treatment for many years. My parents had to buy special footwear and other items. This was well before the introduction of the NHS, and it was a terrible drain on the family's finances. My father was paying medical bills for ten years or more before the introduction of the NHS, so can I ask the people who deride this wonderful hospital system this country has, and very often call for its disbandment, to think again. Sit back and consider the consequences, should this ever happen. I will say that my brother's injuries never seemed to bother my father, but perhaps I was too young to understand things as they really were. A tragedy of this nature would have driven a lesser man to drink, but his family was his main consideration, so drowning his sorrows would never have been an option from his point of view.

A DESERVED DRENCHING

A good part of Cottage View was taken up by a cabinet-maker and joinery works. The workshop took up an area beginning from the rear of the Spread Eagle pub to about halfway along the street to Mrs Russell's house. There was the usual set-up for this kind of operation with the wood machines on the ground floor of the building; the carpenters' workbenches situated on the first floor, and a staircase at each end of the building, serving the carpenters' workshop.

In the days of open fires, households were always on the lookout for scrap timber or off-cuts, and at times, I was asked by my mother if any of this valuable commodity was available from the workshop. For some reason I thought that it was great fun to stand at the bottom of the stairs and give the carpenters a lot of cheek. More often than not I would get away with it; but not this time. Today was to be my learn a lesson day! A bucket of water, long since placed in readiness, lay in wait for the cheeky little sod from across the road. One word was all it took, and — WHOOSH!! — down it came from the top of the stairs; one bucket of cold water all over yours truly! I had to return home soaking wet and tell my mother who did this to me. My mother was across the road in a flash to get the facts. She got the facts alright; not only of this event, but also of my bad behaviour in the past towards these men. I was punished of course. I had to remain indoors for a long time; a punishment that I hated. But that was the end of me giving lip to the carpenters! I would always be punished if I had offended in any way, but my mother would always stand by me if I had been ill-used.

I spent a lot of my time playing in the next street in the company of Vic Spry; a lifelong pal of mine.

A certain lady in Guildford Street had taken a dislike to me, and this day it blossomed into verbal abuse. "Clear off back to your own street and tell your mother to give you a proper pair of shoes to wear" she said. Feeling, and I am sure, looking very crestfallen, I arrived back home and gave my mother the lady's message.

"Are you sure that is what she said?" asked my mother.

"Yes Mum" I replied.

"You wait here" cried Mum.

I never waited of course. I followed my mother to witness the confrontation. My mother stood only five feet three inches, but she would take on anyone; man or woman. This lady never stood a chance; she saw my mother coming and ran into her house. My mother judged this as an act of a guilty person, and ran in after her. She took this person to task in no uncertain terms, and I had no more bother from the lady when playing in the street. My mother could be very fiery, but it was in her nature to help anyone in need. I have witnessed her kindness to others many times. I was fortunate to live in an area where such kindness would have been reciprocated.

CHRISTMAS AND HOLIDAYS

I feel sure that all the children in the Christian world, will have learned in school the true meaning of Christmas. We were not a churchgoing family, and never have been, but if I ever had to look for role models in kindness and thought for others, then I would have looked no further than the street where I lived. Our house was always decorated for Christmas with paper chains, some home-made, a bit of holly and maybe a cheap Christmas tree from the market. I have no wish to bore you with the story told so many times by the elderly, you will have heard it, I am sure, but I will jog your memory. "All I got for Christmas when I was a kid was an apple, an orange, a few nuts and a new penny." I wonder who the first person was to tell that story? I was always excited at Christmastime, and I really looked forward to hanging my stocking up. My mother made our Christmas pudding well in advance, and my father always made the pickled onions. The centrepiece for the Christmas table was the good old chicken. My parents always made a special effort for us kids at Christmas, and the three of us had one present each. I can never remember the kids in Cottage View having expensive toys as presents; finances would just not allow it. For a change my parents would have a glass of beer with their meal, just because it was Christmas. The brewers would never have became rich if they had to rely on my parents using their pubs. My father's mother was a little too fond of her tipple, and I think that my father made up his mind that he would not follow in her footsteps.

At this time of year, the shops in Arundel Street and Commercial Road did make a really good job of decorating their stores for the festive season. Sad to say that the effort that the multinationals make of decorating their stores today is really abysmal.

An experience that I would have loved to have had as a child, was to have travelled away with my parents on holiday. As a child, of course, I never realised or understood that their was such a thing as a week's holiday. Finances at this time would have put the idea of a holiday out of the question. The burden of medical bills was really causing problems for my parents, and to add to their anxiety my father had just lost his job at the fishmongers and was to be out of work for a number of weeks, as were many other men at this moment in time. Not all bad news though; after many visits to the Labour Exchange, he had the offer of employment in Portsmouth dockyard. The work was in the plumbers' shop of the Department of Works. He remained in the dockyard until his retirement and he was awarded the BEM for his services. A regular job at last. It wasn't a lot to ask for, was it?

SEARCH PARTY

Very often in summertime, the mums in Cottage View would organise a get-together on the beach near to Clarence Pier. Most would take sandwiches, etc., for a picnic. It made a nice little change for us kids; we would normally have played in the street. Not that I cared one jot, as I was always happy in the street; it was my world. Walking was the order of the day, and the families would meet in an agreed part of Clarence, not too far away from the public toilets. I can never remember going to the South Parade end of the beach; maybe it was too far to walk! Quite a number of the families would enjoy a day out in this way; mostly mums with their children, and sometimes a couple of dads.

Normally everything would go well and to plan, but on this day I had decided that I would take a stroll on my own. For some reason I decided that I would take a stroll home. Kids will always take these irrational decisions without a care for the consequences. To walk home from Clarence Pier to Cottage View was no mean feat for a kid of my age, but all that I had in my mind was to walk home. I arrived at my house and sat on the doorstep. Back on the beach, it was a little while before I was missed. When the search for me began, a number of people offered their services to look for me; with no luck. It was then that the police were called. I do not think that the passage of time means anything at all to very young children. I was still sitting on the doorstep when a policeman turned the corner into the street, and upon seeing me, quickened his step. I raced back through my mind; I hadn't done anything untoward; not recently anyway. The policeman stopped and asked if I was Mickey Franckeiss?

"Yes" I replied.

"Everybody is out looking for you. Where have you been?" he

said.

"I walked home from the beach" was my reply.

"Good God" he said. He was a little shocked, I think. It was a bit like a Dickens' scene with Mr Bumble. "You little bugger. Do you know your mother has been crying?" he exclaimed.

Needless to say, Flo Faithwaite was the person designated by me when I was asked by the bobby who would look after me until my mother returned.

The other mums and children were to return shortly, as did my mother. I heard comments such as "Put the little sod to bed" and "If he were mine I would keep him in for a month." I believe that my mother was too pleased to see me safe and sound to want to do any of those suggested punishments. I was reminded of this misdemeanour a few times by the neighbours. Was I right in thinking that they wanted me to remain missing? It is said that you are famous in your life for fifteen minutes; maybe that was my fifteen minutes!

By a strange quirk of fate, my own six-year-old son went missing on a beach when we were holidaying in Canada, and we had to call the police. Our son was found after an agonising hour of searching. My wife and I were worried sick. Do you think that this was some form of punishment for my misdeeds in my earlier life? I fully understand now how my mother must have felt when I decided to go walkabout.

TEA AFLOAT

It would be very odd indeed if this narrative did not give the Navy a mention, with Portsmouth being the naval city that it is. All of my family were either sailors or marines.

One of my father's younger brothers, Leonard, had joined the Navy; his ship at this time was the *Iron Duke*, which was berthed at the South Railway Jetty in the dockyard. As is often the case "Jolly Jack" was laying on a party for the crew's children. My Uncle Len, at this time a Petty Officer PTI, invited my sister Kathleen and myself to the ship's party. To my sister's amazement, I can remember being taken to this party; I may have been only five years old at the time. As per usual, when you are guests of the Royal Navy, everything possible was done to make your visit a happy one. We were all waited on by the crew, and entertained from the moment that we stepped on board ship.

A long time has passed by since my sister and I had such a wonderful time on board HMS *Iron Duke*. That memory has always stayed with me.

Another memory really has nothing to do with my mind, but it is the memory of a ship's 'aroma'. Perhaps any ex-sailors that may read this will understand when I ask, is this true? Does a ship have an aroma all of its own? I can remember a very cosy feeling when walking on board. The aroma is difficult to define. It is something that I have never experienced in my life before! For some reason I have never asked a sailor this question. I think that it is time that I did, it is an interesting thought.

Uncle Len was to change ships just prior to the beginning of World War Two, and this move was to end this dear man's life. More of that later in this story.

MORE MISCHIEF

I got up to mischief, as did many of my friends, and I realise now that we were very much out of order, but let me make it clear, never was vandalism involved or downright nastiness to the elderly. Trouble was kept to a minimum by a policeman on his beat, and also my father had very strict rules. If I received a clip round the ear from my father, then I knew that I had deserved it. Very rarely did my father lift his hand to his children.

Gingerbread was a favourite bit of mischief for our gang. A piece of string tied door to door across the street would be fixed up, then we would knock both doors simultaneously; wait to see the result, and then run like the devil. We would also move a bicycle from outside one house and place it outside the front of another. All relatively harmless fun, but still a nuisance to the people of the area.

Saturday mornings would see some of the scallywags and I spending time going up and down in the lifts of the LDB on the corner of Arundel Street; another fine building laid to waste by the bombing. The manager and his staff would only put up with us for a very short time, and then out we would go, ejected from the store and quite rightly so!

The 2d. picture club on a Saturday afternoon was a must for me, providing that I had the tuppence. A paltry sum by today's standards, but nevertheless not always easy to come by. Our picture club was at the Rialto Cinema in Arundel Street. If I didn't have the two pennies for official entrance, I would try to bunk in the fire exit door which came out into Church Path. Management were well aware of this little scam, and it was a proper cat and mouse game. You had to have a friend to help you gain entry in this illegal fashion, and I will tell the world that very often the friend that helped me in this way was Vic Spry. There you are Vic, I said that I would make you famous. I liked to watch the cowboy films, that is when there was not a good scrap going on in the aisle! I think that the kids liked to act out the scenes that were on the screen; always the noise was deafening. Gene Autry, Johnny McBrown and others of that era I really enjoyed. Always the greasy baddies eventually got their comeuppance; that in itself is always a good lesson for young children to take in. I can recall being thrown out of the Rialto two or three times, but I can assure you that it was only for boisterous behaviour, nothing more than that. The staff's action must surely have been justified!

ANOTHER ARRIVAL

April 4th 1937. Another date that is lodged in my memory, as this is the day that my brother Brian was born. I am very glad that he arrived on the scene, as when he became old enough, he took over my title of little sod. My mother had been taken to St Mary's Hospital for her confinement, and Mrs Spry, Vic's mum, had volunteered (as always) to take care of me at her house in Guildford Street. Neighbours were so good and kind in those days. It was on a bright sunny day that my brother was born. I was sitting on the pavement with my pal Vic, and Mrs Spry handed us both an orange, and as she did so informed me that I had a baby brother! I have no idea of my reaction to this news; probably my main interest would have been the orange.

I am fairly certain that the street photograph on the front cover would have been taken at this time, and my age would have been the same as Vic's; four years and a bit. It was to be eleven years before I was photographed again. I wonder what the reason was?

As you have probably realised whilst reading this part of my story, Mr and Mrs Spry were always very kind to me, and I am very pleased to be able to put this on record. Their house in Guildford Street was a little smaller than the house in which I lived in Cottage View. It was always sparkling clean and a real happy home for her large family of five children; namely, Doris and Donald, Gwen, Victor and Raymond; and that kind lady still had time to take care of me. This was Pompey in the thirties!

HAIRCUTS AND FAG CARDS

As I have already written, there was a great variety of shops and services to be found in Arundel Street in the thirties, and one of the services that our family and many others used, was Adams the barbers. His business was next door to the Cat and Dog meat shop that, at one time, was called the Duke of Edinburgh, a Brickwoods pub. Next to a meat shop, did someone mention Sweeney Todd? Mr Adams' shop did good business cutting the children's hair, as well as many dockies who would drop in on their way home. I remember him as a friendly man, and always very patient. I hated having my hair cut, and I would wriggle about and fidget. Old Adams certainly earned his threepence! His business continued into the fifties, and I sincerely hope that he had a long and happy retirement.

"Please can I have the fag card Mister?" — a very familiar request to be heard outside the tobacconists at this time, and very often a fag card would come your way. I always made a point of hanging around the tobacconists on a Friday, hoping to waylay the many dockyard men who had been paid that day and were calling in for their cigarettes. Many different types of cards were to be had at this time, but my special prize would be a silk flag; not always easy to come by because they came with a dearer brand of cigarette; and also they were so attractive that the purchaser liked to keep them for his own collection. The collecting of these cards was a very serious business, as well as a good pastime. Swapping cards with your pals was very nearly an art. I lost my very good collection when our house was bombed.

SCHOOL AND TRUANCY

My introduction to school life was to me, to say the least, quite a shock. I think that it was the discipline part of my new experience, that will have sown the seeds of my disenchantment with school life. Relatively speaking, I consider that I was a fairly well-behaved youngster, with not a little respect for my elders. I will never have any respect for bullies, especially those who are in a position of trust.

Came the day for me to begin my school life in the infants of Arundel Street School. My mother had spruced me up, and it was time to go. We walked to the bottom of Landport Street, into Church Path by the Dial pub, and then on to school. It did not seem to me to take long on my first walk to school; maybe it was my feeling of apprehension of wondering what to expect. My mother walked with me across the playground and on into the classroom. The teacher was already sitting at his desk. My mother introduced herself and me. I was shown where to sit and my mother walked out of the room. I can remember no words of encouragement from my new teacher. My memories of starting school are few and not very happy ones. From the outset the teacher was to stamp his authority on the newcomers. The three hours till dinner time seemed to me to take an age, and the thought of having to return in the afternoon filled me with doom and gloom. We were not allowed to talk in class; this I expected for the first day, but in a short time I had either forgotten this rule or ignored it at my peril. I was caned on my hands at least three times during my first week. If I could name this bully I would. This person distilled in me a great dislike of school when I should have been encouraged to enjoy it.

A plan was forming in my young mind to avoid going to school as much as possible. I now know that I am talking about truancy; a word that I had never heard of in those far-off days. The end of my back garden is adjacent to Moorings Way Infants' playing field, and retired as I am, I have time to watch the children at play and their outside lessons, and it gives me great pleasure to see how happy the children and the teachers are. What a staggering contrast to my early schooldays. I cannot help thinking that had I had teachers of this calibre, my whole education would have taken a different course. I suppose the buildings themselves would also make a difference to first impressions. In my opinion, Arundel Street School was like a Victorian workhouse compared to the modern little school in Moorings Way. I am more than convinced that the bad start that I had to my education, retarded the learning process from the beginning.

The school beadle was at our house many times, and my mother and father were at their wits' end wondering what to do to resolve the situation. What a fool I was, and how thoughtless to put my parents through this misery. I hear some of you saying that the answer to this problem would have been a good thrashing! My father, I am happy to say, was not of that ilk. My reason for behaving in this way, was through the harsh treatment I received from my infants' teacher. In spite of everything, I was still to be at Arundel Street School at the outbreak of World War Two.

WAR AND DEATH

A war that was to change my whole life and many other millions of people all over the world — World War Two. Trouble had been brewing up for a long time before the actual declaration of war with Germany. All the talk of war and peace in our time, etc., was of course all unbeknown to me, as after all I was an innocent child of six and a half years old. It was whilst walking to school one morning, with a friend who obviously knew more about current affairs than I did, that the subject of Hitler and war was brought to my attention. After a brief discussion, we decided there and then that should that 'evil being' come our way, he would be 'bashed up'.

Immediately that war was declared, preparations were put into motion for the protection of the civilian population. The building of the air-raid shelters were the preparations closest to me. Not all houses in the area were large enough to accommodate a brick or an Anderson shelter in the yard. Consequently the answer was to build large brick air-raid shelters in the streets. This type of shelter was for communal use, and one stood at the top of Cottage View in Railway View. I could be corrected, but I estimate that the size of the communal shelter would have been approximately thirty feet by eight feet. Built into the structure was an escape hatch of loose bricks. A slatted bench ran the whole length of the shelter on both walls. The description of the air-raid shelter that I have given you, is about all that there is to say regarding the amenities of these shelters. It was very cold indeed to sit and wait for the all-clear siren to be sounded.

A great deal of the air raids occurred at night, and people will have left their beds to spend the rest of the night in these places. When I hear of present-day, highly-paid sportsmen complain of stress, my mind always returns to the war years in Portsmouth. I wonder if these people complained of stress? Of course not! It was sterner stuff that they were made of!

An added discomfort was the seepage of water that ran into the brick and Anderson shelters, and very often it would be wet feet for everyone.

Arundel Street School had a shelter in the playground, and during daylight raids, many hours were spent sitting in the shelter, with the teacher doing his best to make his charges take their minds off of the goings on outside. Not an easy thing to do, as the sound of the air raid going on all around us, was quite frightening.

For the younger person reading this narrative, I will describe the make up of the Anderson shelter. They were made of extremely strong corrugated iron, prefabricated and bolted together sections to form something similar to a six feet square shed, and the whole thing would be sunk about three feet into the ground. Once again water penetration was a serious problem, and added to this, condensation ran down the roof and sides. It made the shelters uncomfortable and damp. It is no wonder that some people chose to take a chance, by remaining in the house and sitting in the cupboard under the stairs. The Faithwaites had a small brick shelter built in their backyard. I know this because I took shelter on a number of occasions in this shelter. I also have vivid memories of it being built, because when the brickies took time off for their dinner break, I would lay a few bricks for them, just as a favour to help them along. For some reason they dismantled the bricks that I had so carefully laid!

The landladies of the Spread Eagle public house, very kindly allowed people to use the pub cellar as an air-raid shelter, for which many people were grateful. Thanks a lot Edna and Auntie.

I have no wish to dwell on tragedy, but as I am writing this part of my story about Portsmouth in wartime, it is important to write about an event that happened far away from home, yet it affected the people of Portsmouth so tragically. I have mentioned earlier the sad loss of my Uncle Len. He had changed ships just prior to the outbreak of war, from HMS *Iron Duke* to HMS *Royal Oak*. The *Royal Oak* was sunk by enemy action at Scapa Flow in the Orkney Isles on the 13th–14th October 1939. My uncle managed to reach shore in spite of his injuries, which were burns and oil inhalation, but died in hospital. He was laid to rest on Lyness Island. I had seen my mother cry before when my brother was so seriously injured, but that was the only time up until now. School had finished and I arrived home, and as usual my first words were "What's for tea?" My poor mother was crying as she had just received the news of my Uncle Len's death. Quietly she told me the sad news, and for a long time our house was in a state of mourning. A wonderful twenty-seven-year-old man had gone out of our family forever. Many people of Portsmouth were to grieve over the loss of this ship and so many of her crew. It is of little comfort I know, but our family were not alone in their sorrow.

Len was the first of the Franckeiss family to give his life in World War Two. John Edward Franckeiss, who was a sergeant in the Royal Air Force, died whilst training for aircrew in Canada in 1943. His name is on the Roll of Honour in Edinburgh Castle, Scotland.

DEDICATION:

Len Franckeiss, RN.
Died aged twenty-seven.

John Franckeiss, RAF.
Died aged twenty.

In 1939, Uncle Len lost his life when the Royal Oak *was sunk by enemy action. He was a petty officer.*

In 1943, John died in an air crash in Canada, whilst training for promotion from sergeant.

GOODBYE COTTAGE VIEW, HELLO NEW FOREST

The air raids on Portsmouth were growing progressively worse, in that they were more frequent and far more concentrated. But Hitler had only just begun to vent his feelings on Portsmouth, and that evil bastard still had not finished his business with my family. This night yet another raid on Portsmouth; again, a night-time air raid, and once more we were woken from our sleep by (moaning minnie) the air-raid siren. So it was out of bed, get dressed into winter clothing, and the whole family would proceed to the communal air-raid shelter as quickly as possible. Many families preferred to spend the night in houses outside of Portsmouth, and travelled by bus to these houses very early in the evening. I would imagine that they had a better night's sleep than those that stayed. Another option was the tunnel shelters on Portsdown Hill. I was never to go to either of these places, so consequently I am unable to give further details.

This night for our family, was to prove very different. Usually after an air raid, providing the raid had finished in the early hours of the morning, it may be possible to have a few more hours' sleep, or lie in your bed before daybreak. The action seemed to be very near to us during this particular night raid, and after the all clear had been sounded, we were to see the reason for this. On the way back to our house, we found ourselves walking over large amounts of rubble. The nearer we got to our house, so the amount of rubble increased. Our house, although still standing, had been very seriously damaged. The joinery works opposite our house had been burning fiercely, and the roof and woodwork on the front of our house had been burned away. Any thoughts of bed were soon pushed out of our minds. A house for the family was found very quickly in Catisfield Road, Milton (either No.30 or 32). My mother always referred to Milton as the posh district of Portsmouth; maybe because the houses were not as old as those in Fratton.

Air raids were to become a part of life in Portsmouth. I do not wish to imply that they were accepted, but they had to be tolerated. Personally I began to fear these raids more and more, and I believe that my mother realised this was happening to me. I can remember my mother holding me close to her and placing her hands over my ears. My reactions to the air raids grew steadily worse, and I think that recognising this, made up my mother's mind to have me evacuated. I was never asked what I thought of the idea. I was to go and that was that. I have written an account of my life as an evacuee, and I will say quite honestly, that the experience did me no harm whatsoever. Yet again in my life, fortune was to smile upon me as I was taken in by a wonderful lady in her little thatched cottage, which was tucked away in the small village of Wood Green in The New Forest. A heartfelt thanks to the people of this village; they were a wonderful group of people. Perhaps you would like to read my first book, *I Never Cried*, which is an authentic account of my evacuation, written by yours truly. It is printed and published by A. H. Stockwell.

Just as a reminder to some of you, and I feel sure an eye-opener to the younger reader, I will list here a number of foods that were rationed in wartime England. These are accurate amounts of civilian entitlement of food for one person per week:

> Bacon and ham, 4oz, if available.
> Sugar, 8oz.
> Tea, 2oz.
> Red meat, 8 pence worth.
> Butter, 2oz.
> Sweets, 2oz.
> Cheese, 1oz.
> Margarine, 4oz.
> Cooking fat, 4oz.
> Dried eggs, 1 packet.
> Onions, 1lb per person.

Oranges, if available, could be bought by expectant mothers only. Clothes were also rationed. So many coupons were allowed for each item, and it was not such an unusual event for a number of these items to be unavailable. The people just had to accept this horrible situation.

A NEW BEGINNING

I returned to Portsmouth from evacuation just prior to D-day; a momentous time for England and her Allies, and especially for my home town. The surrounding area of Portsmouth was taken up by serving men of all nationalities; masses of equipment and many thousands of men, waiting for the signal for the invasion of Europe to begin.

One of these brave men was my mother's brother, my Uncle John. He was a Royal Marine gunner, and his home was with his sister in Milton Road; our new home. John had been on standby at Southwick for over a week. Being so near to home, the temptation to pay his sister a visit proved to be too great. So he broke all the rules and paid a sneak visit to our house, and why not? Without wishing to be too dramatic, I will just say that this might have been his last chance to see his family. Thousands of those dear men did lose their lives at the outset of the invasion. Before leaving our house, he asked me if I was broke. Of course I was, and so he gave me all of his loose change. He had already been issued with his occupation money and, against all the rules, let me have a quick look. They were notes, a fraction smaller than the old pound note, with the national flags of England, France and the USA displayed on the face.

My dear Uncle John fought his way from the Normandy beaches to the heart of Berlin. Good fortune smiled on him, and he lived throughout this hazardous time and came back home to us after his demob. He had in later life, the desire to emigrate to Australia and did so under the auspices of the £10 Assisted Passage Scheme, and lived there until his death in 1993.

YET ANOTHER MOVE

I have not mentioned the fact that I first saw the new family home on my return to Portsmouth, but Hitler had not quite finished venting his anger on the family, because shortly after moving to Catisfield Road in Milton, the house sustained air-raid damage. It was the result of a land mine exploding and wiping out the corner of Locksway Road. It had been packed with high explosives, and did far more damage than the average bomb would do. This meant of course, that once again my family had to move, and the new address was 125 Milton Road.

The house stood opposite Bowler Avenue. Oddly enough another land mine had dropped into the very corner of Kingston Prison's grounds. If it had have dropped a few more feet on the outside of the yard's walls, then the whole of Bowler Avenue and a bit more of the immediate area would have been destroyed. As it was the terrific force of the explosion blew away the prison walls; wiped out the Airspeed Social Club, and a number of houses in Bowler Avenue. I did see the crater left by the land mine; it was always half-filled with water, and I would spend a lot of my time catching newts that lost no time in colonising the water.

Just like the newts making use of the land mine crater, the children of the area lost no time in making use of the bomb site as a play area. It was a dangerous thing to do, but I can quite honestly say that of all the children who regularly played on the bomb site, I cannot recall any injuries or accidents. We played in the gardens of the bombed houses, and what I would like to mention, is the notice that I had taken of the plant life that still flourished in the unattended gardens, as if trying to tell the war-weary people of Portsmouth that all was not lost, and try and look to the future. Also I think that it is a tribute to the people that once lived in those houses and carefully cultivated their little gardens. What a joy to them it would have been, if like me they would have seen it all flowering and coming to life once again in spite of everything.

On the corner of Bowler Avenue and Milton Road, stood the now empty and bomb-damaged house that served 'prewar' as the prison governor's residence. It was a very large house and also had a large and beautiful garden; no doubt tended by the convicts in Kingston Prison. The inmates of the prison at this time however, were naughty sailors, as it was being used as a Naval detention barracks. Back to the garden; many soft fruits flourished in this one-time beautifully kept garden. Gooseberries, blackcurrants, redcurrants, strawberries, loganberries, cultivated blackberries, apple trees, pear trees, a mulberry tree and a truly lovely walnut tree; all of these cropped wonderfully well. The old prison governor's house; very nice to look at, and full of character, had been damaged by the bombing, but with good planning and careful renovation this fine old house would still have been an asset to the area. Unfortunately it was to become yet another victim of madcap planning. The house was demolished and the garden was desecrated with trees being torn down, just to make way for a hideous Tarmac car park. What is it about these people, that they want to destroy anything of beauty, just to put yet more money into their overflowing coffers!

A lovely old cottage that stood next door to the Rose In June public house, was also demolished to make way for an awful garage. I should imagine that this cottage was one of the original buildings when Milton was a country area. Further away in St George's Square, Portsea, these so-called planners had the crass stupidity to demolish Brunel's birthplace along with many other wonderful old properties. These properties had escaped the carnage of the terrible air raids on Portsmouth, and had graced the area for over three hundred years, yet in the name of progress (did I say progress?) the wonderful Portsmouth City Council raised their hands in a vote to have these treasures pulled down and lost forever. It is the firm opinion of the people of Portsmouth, that what Hitler and his Luftwaffe failed to destroy, the planners and the developers did for him. How true that is! Here is my definition of a planner/developer — a vandal with a brain implant!!!!

MORE ABOUT MILTON, THE YANKIES AND OTHERS

On my return from the country to live in Milton Road, the first friend that I was to make, was a boy of my age who also lived in Milton Road. His name was John Moore and we were to remain friends for many years. His story is one of courage, and I will begin this chapter with his story.

Maybe some of you will recall the period in the late forties when poliomyelitis was claiming its victims. A terrible disease of the spinal cord, that normally began with a fever and caused paralysis. My dear old pal John, had the incredible bad luck to be struck down by this disease, which meant that for the rest of his life he would be confined to a wheelchair. He was fourteen years old; maybe younger. John was one of the kids in the area who was always being blamed for any misdeeds; whether guilty or not! The cry would go up "It's that Johnny Moore." Sometimes it would be John, sometimes it was others and sometimes it was me, but I would like to put on record that those same people, that so derided my pal, were deeply sorry when learning of his misfortune, and made it known. John, being the person that he was, always had a chuckle about this ironic situation, and most of all when one of his worst tormentors kissed him, he said "At last I am popular, but for the worst of reasons."

John was always determined from the very beginning, that he would lead as normal a life as possible, despite being confined to a wheelchair, and he did achieve this ambition as, at a later age, he gained employment in the offices of the USG Garage at Hilsea, and married Nancy, a delightful lady. To give you an idea of the stature of this man, and his thought for others, he insisted that I be moved away from his ward in the Infectious Disease Hospital, St Mary's, when I visited him. "Keep away Mick, you don't want what I've got. See you when I get out" was what he said. John knew before he left the hospital, that he would never walk again, and consequently be dependant on other people's help at the outset of his life in a wheelchair. I never heard John whinge or grumble about his misfortune. I will never remember him as disabled. I will remember him as a smiling rascal! He was to die quite young and his wife died soon after him. Maybe it was of a broken heart? It was my privilege to have known them both.

To continue this story, I will endeavour to write of happier memories. Hilsea Barracks, at around the time of 1944–1945, was playing host to the American Army, and a number of the soldiers were to frequent the Rose In June public house, and I believe that on a number of occasions they drank it dry. For some reason they had a liking for English beer. I am not really surprised, as I have tasted their awful lager. People who know about these things, did say that old Bill Whatley did know how to keep his beer. The visits of the GIs turned out to be a bonus for us kids, because we were never backward in asking for chewing gum, badges, and buttons as souvenirs. We harassed these poor men, but never a cross word did we hear!

Strange to relate, or maybe not, the soldiers were rather partial to fish and chips. Did I know of a fish shop that was open at this time of night? Of course I did. "Over in Tangier Road" I told them.

"Would you care to go to the shop and buy fish and chips for us?" they said.

Would I!! I could earn more pocket money in an hour than I could in a week. English pounds and pence, was I believe always a mystery to the Americans, and they would pay well over the odds for cod and chips. I will admit that I had no shame at the time of working this fiddle, but now I am willing to call it 'lease lend'. I will never regret meeting and mixing with the Yanks in Bill Whatley's pub, and I hope and trust that they came through the invasion safely.

Looking for ways to obtain pocket money, was always a preoccupation of mine. One dishonest way of gaining 2d. at the time, was to return beer bottles to Bill Whatley that he had already paid 2d. to another person for the selfsame bottle. All of his empties were in his yard at the side of the pub awaiting collection. Bill realised what was happening and set a trap which I walked into.

He had marked the bottom of the bottles. He called me a cheating little sod! At least I think he said sod!

One of the honest ways of earning my pocket money, was to deliver groceries. By this time I was twelve years old. Mr Shrives was the proprietor of a grocery store on the corner of Bowler Avenue. I had to ride a carrier bike that I only just managed to master. Some customers lived in Cedar Grove, Myrtle Grove, Ebery Grove, Stride Avenue, Hayling Avenue, Langstone Road and Tangier Road. One of the furthest away was the caretaker of a masonic lodge in the Guildhall Square. When all of the deliveries had been made, I helped out in the shop. He was one of three people in the road who owned a car, a Ford Popular, and one of my duties was to clean his car. I worked in his shop all day Saturday, for the princely sum of two and sixpence (twelve and a half pence). The odd tips that I received from the customers for deliveries of 3d. or 6d., made up my day's pay. Old Shrives was a mean bugger; I am told that his ambition was to own a large grocery store at the end of hostilities. By my reckoning if he exploited his other staff as he did me, then he would end up owning Portsmouth! Another trip that I had to make on the carrier bike, was to collect the shop's bacon ration. The wholesalers were in Hyde Park Road, in one of the few buildings that was still standing in that area. That part of Portsmouth had taken a real pounding from the Luftwaffe. The usual amount of bacon that I had to collect was very small, maybe a hock or two and one side of bacon. With these precious rations, I pedalled my way back to Bowler Avenue.

In my life, up until this time, 'lady luck' had smiled on me in the real sense of the word. Coming into contact with three ladies, whom I will mention by name, had made my young life so much better in a world that was going berserk. First of all dear Mrs Faithwaite in Cottage View, who took me under her wing and showed me love. The lovely lady in the village of Wood Green in The New Forest, Miss Gale, who gave up a hell of a lot just to take care of a seven-year-old evacuee from Portsmouth; and a wonderful lady I was to be introduced to by John Moore. Mrs Atlee lived in Bowler Avenue, and I helped her in any way that I could by running errands and doing odd jobs about the house. Her husband was away serving in the Parachute Regiment; one of those brave men at Arnhem. We just seemed to enjoy each other's company right from the very outset. 'Lady luck' had certainly smiled on me!

TWO NEW SCHOOLS

Although I had attended school during my evacuation, my learning had been an all-time low. On my return to Portsmouth, my capability capacity for reading and writing was nil. In fact I was within touching distance of becoming a dunce, and I will only blame myself. Langstone School was to be the school for my area. It was only a short walk to Stride Avenue from Milton Road; I had been walking two miles to school in the country. Ability never counted for anything when placing you in a school at this time; you were placed in a class according to your age. Unfortunately for me at this time, Mr Cooper, whom incidentally was a first-class teacher, was in the process of grooming his class of thirty-nine pupils for the entry exam for Higher Education Schools in Portsmouth. He had no time to waste on me in any kind of special tuition. My learning anything at all would depend entirely on my own capability. The pleasing thing for Mr Cooper was to be the examination results. Almost all of his pupils were to pass and move on to Higher Education. I know of many of my ex-classmates who were very successful in their chosen careers.

Memories of my time at Langstone, are mainly happy ones. On the downside, I have to say that certain members of the class were out-and-out snobs. They had somehow learned that at one time I had lived in Landport, and to these posh Milton boys, whom I would imagine had parents that were fairly well off, meant that I had come from a slum. The clothes that I was wearing were hand-me-downs, and not too good a fit, and I remember my shoes being in a poor state of repair. Learning the meaning of how cruel children can be, was certainly a part of my education at Langstone. Some of the jibes and names that I was called really hurt. Talking of hurt, Mr Ireland certainly knew how to handle the cane. Six of the best from his broad shoulders, across the palms of your hands, gave you something to consider when contemplating some future misdeeds. Two other teachers that I can remember at Langstone were Mr Gibbs and Mr Roberts.

A very big change in education at this time, 1946, saw the introduction of Secondary Modern Schools in Portsmouth under the Education Act. So, once more I had to move on to another school; the freshly-named Copnor Modern School. It was the sixth school that I had attended in eight years, due of course to the outbreak and continuance of World War Two. Copnor was to prove a real eye-opener to me. I had only ever experienced being in one classroom all day with one teacher, who actually specialised in no particular subject, but taught all subjects. May I say very quickly that this did not detract them from being very good teachers. It would be fair to say, that from my point of view, the last year that I was to spend at school, was to be the most productive since starting school in the infants at Arundel Street. Fourteen years of age was my official leaving age.

Copnor to me was quite posh, as I was now attending a school that had a teacher for each subject. This school never provided the handicrafts tuition (or manual). I had to attend yet another school for this tuition, namely Drayton Road. The master was Mr McGavin, and he taught Metalwork, with Woodwork being taught by Mr Pead. Metalwork was to be my subject, although I was never given the choice. The items that I produced turned out very well. Permission was given for me to make two fish slices; one for my mother and the other for my friend Mrs Atlee in Bowler Avenue. Pupils were expected to put some money towards the cost of materials — things never change! Geography, History and English were the subjects that I seemed to enjoy; Maths and Technical Drawing, I endured. To have any chance of doing well at these kind of subjects, ideally an unbroken education would be the answer, which I never had. The master for these two subjects was another Mr Pead, a good master who was good at his subject without any shadow of a doubt. But grasping the two important subjects was beyond me. In an exasperated fashion, he asked me what I proposed doing on leaving school, and I replied that I would try for the trade of a sheetmetal worker, and to my complete embarrassment he told me, and the whole class, that I never had a chance whatsoever of gaining an apprenticeship in that trade. He could have been absolutely right in that assumption, but he maybe should not have made such a scornful reply. Other teachers at Copnor at this time were as follows: Mr Caddy, Mr Gibbs, Mr Thompson, Mr Pearce and Mr Roberts.

Time was drawing near for me to leave school, as I was approaching my fourteenth birthday, and unbeknown to me, my dear father had been making enquiries on my behalf in the building department of Portsmouth dockyard; his place of employment. In all honesty I must say that I was pleased to be leaving school. Maybe I felt this way because of the many disruptions that had occurred during my education, resulting in very little progress in my learning. Copnor had been good for me, without any doubt. My age group would mean that I had just beaten the ruling that fifteen was to be the new age for leaving school. Many friends were leaving like me to start work. I was sad to say goodbye to them; never realising that our paths would cross many times in the future, mainly through the activities we were to pursue — football, table tennis, snooker and being members of youth clubs, and attending local Saturday night hops. A whole new experience lay ahead of me, and I firmly believed that starting work would prove to be the start of my education proper.

WORK AS A LOWLY YARD BOY

"I have some good news for you, Mick." My father had been successful with his enquiries on my behalf, regarding employment in the dockyard. I would be employed pending the outcome of a medical examination. My mother and father were very pleased; I am sure more so for me than for themselves. How fortunate I was to be leaving school and having a job to go to.

The dockyard, derided by so many Portsmouth people, has been for many years an asset to our city and its people, and how sad it is to see it stripped down to the bear bones, and mainly I feel by political squabbles. This was 1947 and I was to leave school with little or no academic achievements, and still have a worthwhile job with prospects. How different it is today when, in some cases, people with university degrees are unable to gain employment. As a wilful teenager, who of course knew all there is to know about life, had without telling my parents, written off making enquiries about joining the Merchant Navy, but my age was against me; sixteen was the minimum starting age. I have often wondered how I would have broken the news to my father, had my application been successful. Hurting my parents' feelings is something that I would have avoided if possible. They have never known of my intentions to join the Merchant Navy. Isn't it strange how happenings such as these change a person's whole life?

My medical examination had to take place in the dockyard, and I was cleared to start work. My place of work was with the Department of Works as a yard boy in the blacksmiths' shop. My father was in the Department of Works working in the plumbers' shop, and had done so since the early thirties. Managing the whole department of carpenters, glaziers, painters, plumbers, bricklayers, smiths, etc., was at this time Mr Northmore. Unbeknown to me at the time, was the fact that by entering the dockyard I would be continuing a family tradition stretching as far back as 1851. My son David is employed at this moment in one of the dockyard stores. I have authentic written proof of my family's association with Portsmouth dockyard.

Mr George Knowles, the leading hand, welcomed me into the blacksmiths' shop, and once more luck was with me, as he was a nice man. He informed me that my first job each day was to clean his office. Many of you may read with interest, or a little humour, that my starting rate of pay would be five and a quarter pence per hour (fivepence farthing); taking home approximately eighteen shillings per week. Not much money for my labours you may say, but it was money that I would receive every week. A skilled blacksmith's wage was the princely sum of three pounds per week.

Once again in my short life, I was to come into contact with some very fine people. I will never be wealthy in the money sense of the word, but my wealth will be in the quality of the people that I have had the good fortune to meet throughout my life. During this narrative I have made a point of naming people, and I will continue to do so. Blacksmiths are as follows: Harry Gill, John Tout, Jack Turvy, Bert Meadows, Arthur Dagwell, Ted Seymour, Terry Lavender, Harry Burrows, Steve Beginek (a French Canadian); hammermen (mates), Bill Groves, Peter Norman, Eddie?, Joe Harrison; chargehand, Tom Feeney and two mechanics, Jim McKean and Alf Davis.

Many of those that I have mentioned were ex-servicemen, and I am bound to say that Harry Gill was the most interesting to talk to. He had been a captain in the Indian Army (Royal Engineers), and had spent many years in that vast country. The stories that he had to tell me left me in wonderment! It is said that education begins when you start work and how true that is.

A man that was to befriend me, and take me under his wing from the day that I commenced my working life in the blacksmiths' shop, was a kind man named John Tout, an ex-World War Two veteran who had survived the battles in the Western Desert, and the beaches of Normandy. John lived with his wife and daughter in Spring Street. His wife's name was Carol. If by chance his wife or daughter should read this, I would be delighted if they were to contact me. Weekends and other spare periods of time, John would spend fishing. He owned a boat with his mooring on

The Hard. Very often I would be invited to go fishing with him and his friend, Lofty. I jumped at the chance. The more time that I spent with John, the happier I seemed to be. But this idyllic and wonderful period of my life was to come to a sudden and tragic end. My dear friend died very young; a tragedy for his wife and family. I attended his funeral in Kingston Cemetery. I am not a person to cry easily, but I am not ashamed to admit that I cried on that day. If I were to model myself in the mould of any man in this world, then it would be in the mould of John Tout. A very, very fine man!

Life for me working in the smithy became very interesting. The skilful way in which the hot metal was beaten into shape for thousands of repairs throughout the dockyard, was a real eye-opener. I visited with a tradesman, in the course of my work, many buildings and areas where maintenance had to be carried out. I can even claim to have worked on HMS *Victory*. No big deal, but on reflection I did think so at the time.

Of course working in the blacksmiths' shop was not the healthiest environment to be working in. Eight forges would normally be alight, and the smoke from these hung in clouds; air conditioning was unheard of. It was a very old building and the only smoke outlet was a louvred lantern light running the length of the roof. Tea for break times would be made from water boiled in the forge in billy cans. Very often condensed milk was considered the best additive. The old camping trick of a chip of wood floating in the billy can to avoid the water tasting of smoke was used, and it worked. A small perk that the smiths and their mates enjoyed at this time, was an issue of a ration of tea in the packet. This is not a widely known fact, but I will vouch for its authenticity. I was to have a ration of tea as well.

Great consideration was given by the men for my wellbeing. "Stand clear Mick" or "Don't lift that on your own" would be some of the many comments made by the men who were my workmates. They could only be called role models in the art of looking after your fellowmen. When the powers disband a group of people such as these, it could only be called sacrilege, and it is still happening as I write! Perhaps it is time now to write of things other than work.

TEENAGE PURSUITS

My leisure interests at this time were table tennis and snooker. As many hours that I could afford to pay for, were spent at the Copnor Temperance Snooker Hall playing these sports. Copnor was a popular venue, and all twelve tables would be occupied very early in the evening, particularly on a Friday evening, so one of our party made a point of being at the club very early; clock on a table, play on his own, and await our arrival. More names: John Potter, Vic Spry, Reg and Morry Stares; just a few of my circle of friends.

Although my friends and I considered the Copnor Snooker Hall to be expensive, between us we just about raked up enough money to pay for the use of the table at closing time (eleven o'clock). A person could hardly write about the snooker hall without mentioning Bert and Gary. Bert was the fat one! Two very nice men, very understanding of youthful behaviour, but at the same time would never stand for any nonsense. One warning only, any further misdemeanours and you were shown the door. A decent cup of tea and a cheese and onion roll could be had at a very fair price and also if, on the odd occasion after clocking you off of the table, you had misjudged your money, you would be trusted until the next time. Many a happy hour in my teenage years I had spent with my friends at this snooker hall.

On reflection, my teenage years will always be regarded by me as the happiest time of my life. Commencing work; meeting new friends; looking forward to, with luck, an apprenticeship as a blacksmith, and not having a care in the world about being called to do National Service. At times like this, with so much going on, I never thought of growing old. It was not in my scheme of things. Did all you ex-teenagers think along these lines?

Being a very keen sportsman, after leaving school I had to find a way of continuing to play football as a team member. Toronto Rangers offered me a trial, which I accepted, but never made the grade. Hillside gave me a chance, but to be in any of their teams at this time, you had to be a bit above average. So the decision was made to apply for membership of Kingston Boys' Club, probably one the best moves of my young life. Reg Stares and myself presented ourselves at the club. Kingston catered for just about everyone in the activities that they provided. Our main interest of course was the fact that the club fielded three football teams. Mr Ernie Bateman was the man that we had to see. He was the second in command to Mr Phillips, club leader. He put us at our ease at once. We had a conducted tour of the club, and I was very impressed with the facilities provided, and the subscription was a shilling a week. What a bargain! And to our delight, we were given a trial for the third football team which competed in the Portsmouth Lads' League. The club was adapted from one of the very large houses in Kingston Crescent. Another plus was that the membership included the fairer sex. A sixpenny hop was arranged for many Saturday nights of the year.

There were very many well-run youth clubs in Portsmouth during my teen years, and I consider the leaders of these clubs the unsung heroes of this very important postwar era. Boredom never came into the reckoning in my youth. There was too much to be involved in. Other popular haunts on a Saturday or Friday night were as follows: Angerstein Hall, Rathgar, The Empress, St Joseph's, The Victory Hall; all with an entry fee of one or two shillings.

A member of the first football team playing for Kingston at this time was Rodney Henwood, a player good enough to sign for Pompey. This was some achievement as Pompey were League Champions and had a really wonderful team.

My life seemed a life of never-ending activity with things always on the boil. Myself and a group of friends were very keen cyclists, and a regular Sunday run would be a trip to The New Forest. My old bicycle was very nearly at its end, at least as for being safe to ride. My father very kindly agreed to be my guarantor for a new bicycle, which I purchased for two shillings and sixpence per week. The price of this new machine was a colossal nineteen pounds; just over nineteen weeks' wages.

Unlike today's situation regarding apprenticeships for school leavers, employers were more enlightened and had the good sense to look to the future; making sure that tradesmen would always be available. After all, five years' training is a very small part of a working man's life. All of my friends had the good sense to be serving apprenticeships, and all became good tradesmen. From 1980 onwards, a certain lady prime minister put into being the idea of scrapping apprenticeships, and the business community rubbed their hands with glee. But the wheel has turned full circle. At the time of my writing, the very same people are now bemoaning the fact that the building industry alone in southern England have vacancies for thirty thousand tradesmen which they are unable to fill!

The idea of camping at weekends and bank holidays was suggested, and we really began in earnest to beg or borrow the camping equipment that we needed for the new venture. I am happy to say that we were successful; our main prize, and to our joy, was the permanent loan of a bell tent, two smaller tents, and clever Vic made a prefabricated spit.

All the equipment that was needed was somehow carried on our bicycles. We had gained permission in advance to camp in a field at Old Bursledon; a beautiful spot on the edge of a copse; now sadly built on. Fresh water we were able to use from a spring that trickled out from the side of a bank in the lane; crystal clear and very cold. For those of you that might know the location of the Fox and Hounds public house in Bursledon, you will have a very good idea of our camp site. We were only about five hundred yards further on down the lane. Of course our arrival was something fresh and new to the local talent, and we were never short of female company. Very often our camping would coincide with the village hop; a bonus from our point of view. A very attractive girl, the daughter of the pub landlord, visited our camp. The main attraction for her was Kenny Atkins, who I am bound to say had the looks of a film star. Sad to say dear Ken died a short while ago.

The main dormitory was the bell tent; laying with our feet to the pole, at least that is how our sleeping positions began during the course of the night. We would move in our sleep. Did I say sleep? Somehow our heads would be under the canvas out in the cold night air. Still, we had breakfast to look forward to. Note I never said cooked breakfast. Well it was cooked, of course, after a fashion. What would camping be without the good old breakfast fry up? Bear with me a moment whilst I describe our fine first meal of the day: three or four tins of beans, warmed in the pot to a smoky perfection; sausages, fried, unpricked and exploding all over the place; streaky rashers of bacon, fried to a crispness to be transformed into pork scratchings and soggy fried bread. At this stage of the proceedings the cooking fat had become really black, with all kinds of bits of this and that hanging around in it. Now it was time for the frying of the eggs. Every yolk broken on entry to the pan and the whites turned grey. Surprisingly though all the food that I have just described was always scoffed down to the last morsel. We were all young and could eat a house! Strong tea, sweetened with that old favourite condensed milk, was our first drink of the day. Those pesky ants were rather fond of condensed milk, and it became a battle of wits trying to keep the open tin hidden.

Reggie and I did attempt the difficult task of making a two-wheeled box trailer to tow behind one of our bicycles. Work began in Reggie's shed at 28 Kimbolton Road, and with the confidence and bravado of youth, we began the task without real planning. The result being a failure. Mistake number one; the wheels were too small and the axle too weak. Come the day to commence the camping holiday, we overloaded our little transport vehicle. Kimbolton Road to Copnor Bridge is no great distance, but our trailer collapsed before we reached that point. Doom and gloom was not our style. Reg and I had a damn good laugh, and still managed to reach our camp site, without the shattered trailer of course. Such is youth! We managed to transport our camping gear down to the town station and onto a train to Bursledon station. It was a fair walk to our camp site, so the porter kindly agreed to lend us his porter's barrow to cart our gear in. A very nice gesture on his part. Another cherished memory of my youth.

Reg and his brother Morry, were great pals of mine, but sadly they both died at a comparatively young age. Many of my friends of prewar days still lived in the Arundel Street area. Making contact was easy as we had a super bus service in Portsmouth. I travelled on the C and D services and they ran as regular as clockwork, unlike today's biscuit tins. People of Portsmouth are of the opinion that a far better bus service operated in wartime Portsmouth. So much for privatization!

KANGAROO SPORTS

As I have already written, in the late forties, youth clubs abounded in Portsmouth, but this fact never deterred three couples from setting up another. Mr and Mrs Alf Rook, Mr and Mrs Harold Swan and Mr and Mrs Bob Taubman, set up and ran a mixed youth club and this takes a vast amount of commitment, but these three couples were blessed with this, as well as an abundance of good humour, kindness and patience. I would like to put on record the superb job of work that they did in setting up and running this club. How the name of the club was named, or arrived at, I have never known. That really does not matter because Kangaroo Sports was a club that it was a privilege to belong to. My membership number was eleven; in fact I was a founder member. Alec Testard, an old school friend of mine, somehow talked me out of leaving Kingston Boys' Club and to become involved with this new venture.

The club room was on the first floor over a garage, standing on the corner of Wharf Road and Commercial Road. The entrance was in Wharf Road and up a flight of stairs. The usual indoor activities were to be had, as well as a snack bar. Of course the fact that it was a mixed club was an added attraction. Many people who met at this club were to marry and have partners for life.

The first year of the existence of the club, a team competed in the Churches' League and I was fortunate enough to be a member of that team. Club night, which was on a Friday, was when team selection for Saturday afternoon would be pinned on the club notice board. Many members were hoping for a place in the team and the team sheet was eagerly awaited. Our first season in this league saw us reach the Churches' League Cup Final, and added to the pleasure of reaching the final, was the fact that the final was to be played at Fratton Park. At this time many local league cup finals were always played in the spring at Fratton Park on mid-week evenings. Later on, a certain Mr Burrows (then Pompey's manager) kindly put a stop to this thrill of a lifetime experience for local players! Of course, being the brash and boastful youth that I was, I urged a number of my workmates and family to come to Fratton and witness the thrashing of Twyford Methodists. Our final was to be played on a Thursday evening in May, and I was to lose many nights' sleep just thinking about it; such was my excitement. Came the great day, and I fulfilled my dream by trotting out onto Pompey's pitch in my club's colours. We lost by three goals to one and I played like a crab! Very disappointed at the time as I was, I realised I had done what many local lads had never done, that was to play at Fratton Park. The team were desperately sorry for our club leaders. To bring a trophy home in our first season would have been a great reward for a good deal of hard work on their part.

A presentation to Alf and Eunice Rook

Once again I have good memories of some fine people, and I would like to conclude this part of the story by naming just a few of the people that I had such happy times with as a member of Kangaroo Sports: Len Pawley, Ron and Alan King, Don Short, Len White, Colin Goble, Roy Cruickshank, Tony Holloway, Geoff Couzins, John Dunstone, Sid Sadler, Den Gallaway, Ted Holdy, Ron Hayward, Bern Fisher, Dave Miller, Bob Mitchell, Bob Taubman Junior, Ernie Hext and many, many more too numerous to mention.

Great days at Kangaroo Sports

A VERY SAD YARD BOY

So far in this narrative I have written mainly of the happy times and good things in my life. However I would imagine, like most people, that I would experience the good times and also times that were not so good. Advice that I will always remember was once given to me by an elderly gentleman, an educated man whom I shall name; Jack Willis, a gentleman that it was my privilege to know. Maybe you would like to be aware of the advice that he gave me? His words were as follows, "Always remember it is not what happens to a person when experiencing a personal tragedy or a calamity, but it is how that person handles the situation and lives through it, and continues his or her life." I had good reason to recall this sound advice later in my life. At this particular time my world was about to collapse!

For a person to say that he was enjoying his work, I suppose seems a bit odd, but the truth is I had no problems whatsoever working as a yard boy, and I firmly believed that a five-year apprenticeship would be mine. One of the blacksmiths that I had worked with more than any other was Arthur Dagwell, a real craftsman and a good instructor. It was on his suggestion that I asked for an apprenticeship. The Admiralty did not do things in this way; the rule was that everyone wishing to be employed as an apprentice had to sit the Civil Service, or Dockyard Examination. Marks gained would determine your choice of trade. Marks on, and above, the pass rate. My confidence on hearing this was at an all-time low. Came the day, and myself and other hopefuls reported to the old Technical College behind the Guildhall to sit the exam. Just let me say that the papers set were way above my education, and consequently I never had an earthly chance of gaining sufficient marks to be accepted as an apprentice. My failing the exam need never have affected my position as a yard boy, but I did have the sense to be looking towards my future, realising that having a trade was of the utmost importance. But to be realistic, it would never have been fair for me to have gained an apprenticeship by the back door method. Even so my leading hand, George Knowles, believed in my ability and considered that I would make the grade given the chance, and with that in mind he did his utmost on my behalf to no avail. To leave the dockyard and the friends that I had made, was a decision that I had to make as soon as possible. Should I remain where I was and be a labourer, possibly for the rest of my life, or move on and do my best to obtain training for a trade? Leave was due to me and this seemed a very good time to take it.

My first port of call at the beginning of my leave would be the Juvenile Employment Office in Victoria Road North. Quite frankly the jobs on offer, such as van boy or counter hand and other similar dead-end jobs, were absolutely out of the question, but the man behind the desk still did his best to persuade me to consider these positions. My second visit to his office was to prove fruitful and, who knows, may have altered the whole course of my life? A general builder wished to employ a young lad as a help to his multi-tradesmen; bricklayers, plasterers, carpenters, painters, etc. His name was William Tilley, and he ran his business from his home in Stanley Avenue, Copnor. It was this address that I had to report to for my interview.

Apprehensive would be the word to describe my feelings as I tentatively knocked on the door of the address given on my employment card. In what seemed no more than a split second, the door opened. My stature was about the average for a lad of fifteen. Mr Tilley, it seemed to me, filled the doorway; he was a very big man. "Are you from the Employment Office? Come on in and let me have a look at you" he said. I had yet to say a word. He was very brusque in his manner, but that appeared more so because of his very big frame. On my way to this interview I had made up my mind that I would 'grasp the mettle' and ask for an apprenticeship, should the opportunity present itself. Without much ado, or any questions regarding my education, I was offered the job of mate to his tradesmen; in other words a labourer. It was at this stage of my interview that I did grasp the mettle, and much to my surprise, I asked Mr Tilley what my chances were of getting an apprenticeship. My nerves were a little stretched at this time, fearing what his reaction would be to my last enquiry. But my fears were unwarranted. "What do you want to be?" he asked. Hesitantly I replied that I would like to be a carpenter. "How would you like to be a painter, as I already have an apprentice carpenter? How would you like it if I gave you a three months' trial run, and if I think that you are suitable, I will have a talk with your father and yourself about the possibility of an apprenticeship. You can start work as soon as you like. The pay is one shilling per hour" is what he said. He held out his hand and that signalled the end of the interview. Thank you Mr Tilley.

This method of a trial run, I feel sure, was the method that the majority of building employers used in my time. Many excellent tradesmen of today began learning their skills in this manner. There was no need for hordes of personnel pretenders as there seems to be at this time. To me, and many of my working colleagues, personnel managers and underlings have always been considered as the unproductives of the business world.

My parents had known nothing of my search for other employment, or of my desire to leave the dockyard. Why I was not more courteous and discussed the dilemma that I was in with my parents, I shall never understand. I am certain that I would have had a sympathetic hearing from the both of them. My mother was the first to hear my news and, like the good mother that she was, was very pleased at my good news, simply because I was. With a little trepidation I waited for my father's return from work. I say trepidation because he had really done his best for me in securing a place for me in the blacksmiths' shop, and I had no wish to appear ungrateful. But my worries were groundless. After I had broken the news to him regarding my new employment, his reaction was true to form. "Well done, Mick. Now we will have to get together and buy some painter's kit" he said. Some of these tools that were purchased at this time I still use. Maybe that sounds like something you have heard before, but it is absolutely true!

SAD GOODBYES AND NEW FRIENDS

The correct thing to do, of course, on my return to the dockyard from leave, was to give notification of my intention to leave their employment. This I did by writing one week's notice. George Knowles understood my reasons for leaving and wished me luck. I was very grateful to him for this seemingly small gesture; it meant so much to me as he had been a real pal in his attitude towards me. The week that I had left to work passed almost too quickly. My waking thoughts over the previous few weeks, had been taken up with my desire to leave the dockyard, but as Friday came into view, little feelings of doubt emerged and of wondering whether I was making the right decision to move on. Friday afternoon was here and it was shake hands time; for me the saddest day of my working life so far. A genuine warm handshake can give a person a very real and personal feeling, and this was happening to me. All the smiths and hammermen (or strikers) and mechanics, in the sincerest manner, wished me good luck.

It did not end with a handshake, because George Knowles called "Come here, you scallywag (he had often given me this name). I have something to tell you." Entirely of their own accord, the men had had a whip-round and wanted me to take this on their behalf. He handed me an envelope which contained money. How could I have thanked these men? Words are just words, and they are, on occasions such as this, entirely inadequate. All had families to care for, but they were generous enough to spare money to give me, a mere yard boy, and it was people of this calibre that I was about to say goodbye to. They certainly made it difficult for me!

Memories of those men that I worked with in the smithy will stay with me forever. How different my life would have been had

I continued working in the dockyard, I shall never know. I had made the decision to leave and embark on another stage of my life.

As per instructions, I reported to Mr Tilley at his home address in Stanley Avenue the following Monday. He employed about twelve people, and being a Monday the majority of his employees would be assembled in his store at the back of his house, prior to proceeding to their places of work. The main reason for being at his house-cum-office was to discuss various aspects regarding the work, and to take instructions. He kindly introduced me to everyone, and at once put me at my ease.

Ernie Payne was to be my first mentor in my new employment. A first-class tradesman, and a very nice man, we were to hit it off from the beginning. His current work was decorating the interior of the governor's mother-in-law's house, and I had to assist. The house was in Fifth Street, off of St Mary's Road. Yet another kind lady who treated me like a son. A very important part of my working day was to endeavour to keep the house clean; not always the simplest of jobs. The reason being, in this case, was that there were other trades working in the house. However the lady of the house appreciated the effort that I put in on this sometimes thankless task, and very often tea and biscuits would be my reward. The freedom of movement, I think, was the most noticeable aspect of my new employment; asked to go here and there on my bicycle by Ernie, to collect materials, etc.; and to me, a cycle ride on a sunny day was a real treat. My first job in the building trade provided me with some happy memories; not the least of which was the kindness shown to me by the governor's ma-in-law.

My introduction to truck pushing was about to begin. Work at Fifth Street was almost completed and my assistance was required elsewhere. "Come to the office in the morning Mick. I would like you to work with the roofer" said Mr Tilley.

Variation of work. This aspect of my new job suited me very well. My new workmate was Percy Harding. Just about everything that a roofer might need was loaded onto the builder's truck. Ladders of course, sand, cement, tiles, slates, bricks, odd lengths of timber, lead, gutter brackets, snow guards, paint, putty, nails, screws and various tools; not any space left unfilled! There were roof repairs to be done in every part of the city, and the normal way to do this work was to push a loaded truck to each place of work. I have never regretted working with all the other trades in the industry, it was to give me a wonderful insight, and a wealth of knowledge, of how work by many other trades had to be completed in the proper manner.

This insight was to stand me in good stead in years to come. By changing jobs I had doubled my earnings from almost six pence per hour to a shilling per hour, and added to which Mrs Tilley, who ran the office and did the wage packets, would often add a couple of bob as a reward for some kind of service rendered outside of my normal work. There was always room in my pocket for an extra couple of bob.

Up to this point in my life, I had had the happy experience of meeting many very nice people, who seemed to me to go out of their way to help me one way or another, and so it continued in this way. Everyone was most helpful during my employment with Mr Tilley. Looming ahead in the not too distant future, was the fact that I would have to do my stint of National Service. More of that later in this story.

My spare time activities carried on pursuing outdoor sports, with youth club life producing an ever-widening circle of friends. Two evenings a week would be set aside for my training runs. Usually the course would be along the shoreline of the Eastern Road. My partner for this very enjoyable activity was Ron Hayward, an old pal of mine who lived in Baffins Road. Maybe coincidence, maybe not, but my youngest son Glen, follows this very same route in his training runs fifty years on! My marriage has been blessed with three sons, and I am glad to say that they all take an interest in sport; perhaps taking after their old man is not such a bad thing after all!

So far I have failed to mention the fairer sex that have crossed my path. Should any of these fair ladies read this, I am sure that they will remember me: Yvonne of Winchester Road, Sylvia of Queens Road, Pearl of Folkestone Road and Margaret of Shearer Road; that will do for now! I will mention one young lady that I admired from afar; her name is Iris. Before I had the courage to approach her with the idea of walking out together, a certain young man by the name of George Fisher stepped in and that was the end of my aspirations regarding that attractive young lady.

As I briefly mentioned a few paragraphs ago, it would not be long before I was called for National Service. The fact that I would be leaving my home again very soon held no fears for me.

I had been an evacuee in World War Two; what better grounding could a person have had? Many of my friends were already serving. Two had been unlucky enough to be posted to theatres of war; one in Korea and one in Malaya. It was a strange kind of peace that we were living in! Doing my National Service held no fears for me, but I preferred not to go to war. I suppose that you might say that I am a pacifist; if politicians want wars, then may I suggest that they go ahead with their colleagues and fight them. My mother's look of anguish will stay with me forever on learning of the death of my dear Uncle Len who lost his life on HMS *Royal Oak*, and of John Edward, who died whilst serving in the Royal Air Force. The ladies in our lives do a great deal of the suffering in wartime!

My time had arrived. The news was brought to me in the form of an official letter, tucked away in a buff-coloured envelope, bearing the magic OHMS. There was no disguising this little package. *"Take this letter with you to your Labour Exchange"* it said. Shortly after this, a trip to Victoria Hall for my medical and interviews. Surprisingly the medical examination was truly just that. Four doctors were in attendance. There was none of this 'bend over, cough, you are in', as is so often described by music hall comedians. Just an added point of interest, we were asked to remove all of our clothes, and had to walk from doctor to doctor with our family jewels swinging in the breeze; no privacy whatsoever! An old school chum of mine, Terry New, a very prominent body builder in the south of England with many titles to his name, happened to be going through the same process as yours truly. I did my best to stand well away from him! His superb body gave me an inferiority complex. I weighed just over nine stone, and compared to Terry I must have looked like a withered reed! He served his time in the RAOC, and I am given to understand that he was actually stationed at Hilsea Barracks. Well, why not? Good luck to him. He is now in Canada and the owner of a gymnasium; I wish him well.

In theory, in the event of your medical examination being a success, you had the option of serving in the Army, Air Force or Navy, but in reality there was no choice at all. You were asked to nominate a service on one of a number of forms that you were asked to complete. I took the chance of writing first, second and third choice all Royal Air Force, and somehow it did the trick. So it was Air Force here I come.

In less than two weeks, I had received my instructions and travel warrant to report to RAF Padgate via Warrington, Lancashire, May 1st 1951. It was time to leave my home again, but this time more of a man than an infant. No fuss or bother, my mother said goodbye to me at the door of 125 Milton Road and I was on my way to the town station for a train to London and then on to Warrington.

Me on leave, 1952 — Reg Stares, top right;
Ken Atkins, seated first left, now passed on.

The RAF was a completely new world; a type of life that a civilian would never have dreamed of. I have already written a book describing my experiences in the Royal Air Force. It is published by A. H. Stockwell of Ilfracombe, Devon. I need only write here that I did my stint as a National Serviceman. My postings were all in England, and I am very happy to say that I never fired a gun in anger! It was an experience that I shall never forget, and I am absolutely convinced that it did me no harm whatsoever. In fact I feel sure, quite the reverse.

Needless to say that keeping in touch with my many friends in Portsmouth during my service time, was very important to me. Hitchhiking home was fairly easy during National Service, providing of course you were in uniform. I always seemed to be able to manage to reach Pompey in good time for an evening out with the lads; normally on a Friday. My first port of call would be the Spread Eagle in Arundel Street, and Edna or Auntie would give me the info as to the whereabouts of my friends, and it would be no surprise to me to be told the Labour Club in St John's Road. The hop took place in the upstairs hall. The entrance fee two shillings and well worth it!!

THE NATURAL WAY OF THINGS

Among my group of friends was a certain Ken Bundy, who lived in Lucknow Street in Fratton. It was whilst on one of my periods of leave that I happened to be with Ken, when unexpectedly I met his niece. We were introduced and I found out that her name was June Bundy. Never did I imagine that this chance meeting would lead to a lifelong partnership. June's family lived in Netley Street, quite near Cottage View, so I would say that we may have seen each other very often in our young lives. Eighteen months is the difference in our ages. I am the eldest, I hasten to add!

On the beach without me, away on National Service: John Potter, Ken Bundy, June, Vic Spry, Reg Stares, Ray Spry and Peter.

On my return to camp, I lost no time in writing to June and this was to be the first of very many letters. Now I know that this is a very unromantic thing to say, but I really do not remember what I managed to write in so many letters. Could it have been that I was falling in love? There you are ladies, men do have romance in their soul after all!

June and me — about 1952

Leave periods took on a whole new meaning to me, mainly of course due to the fact that I would be spending my leave with June. Well, becoming engaged to be married was the next logical step, and we did this after a very level-headed discussion. When hearing of my intentions, my future wife's father was far from happy. Had I had been in his position I would have objected to the idea as well. Like a good many of my age group, downing pints of beer and becoming a nuisance to the immediate company, seemed the macho thing to do, and I fully understood that his concern was for his daughter's welfare. Whatever June said to her father to persuade him that we were a suitable match, certainly put him and I on a level footing, although I know that June's father did have reservations about my suitability, but from the time that he accepted the fact that June and I had made up our minds to marry, then his support for us knew no bounds. To me, Lily and Arthur were to become super in-laws.

My next priority was to save enough money for an engagement ring, which I had planned to buy when next on leave. A bit of a knees-up was arranged to celebrate our engagement, and the Baffins Inn in Tangier Road was our venue. It is a fact that you ladies, when meeting their future in-laws for the first time, are a little nervous. The comments that I received from my family regarding my bride-to-be were really pleasing. Our parents were on Christian name terms at once! Never has there been a cross word between our two families. Our mothers became friendly enough to work together as tea ladies for an engineering company called CJC, based in Farlington. How lucky we both were to have such fine parents supporting us.

Like so many National Servicemen, demob was my main consideration and, sad to say, on reflection of course, it clouded a person's mind with regard to work and prospects in civvy street, as opposed to work and prospects if one remained in the service. Working in the building trade is not the best of places to be employed if you are looking for advancement. Having to do moonlighting for a very long time, as I did in the fifties and sixties, to be able to afford a mortgage, is a good way of describing the very limited earning potential I and many others were experiencing in the building trade at this time. How I made the decision to leave the RAF is still a mystery to me. Probably knowing that very soon I would be spending a good deal more time with the woman that I loved and would soon marry, completely blinded me to the practicality of life in civvy street. Throughout one's life decisions are made, some prove to be the right course of action and a percentage are sure to be wrong, but that is what life is all about. It is impossible to turn back the clock; one can only wonder what might have been?

Needless to say, I had made some very good friends in the RAF, and the fact is that I still keep in touch with a couple of them to this day. It was time to shake hands and say goodbye to RAF Debden and the RAF.

My home was waiting in Milton Road, much to the chagrin of my brother Brian, as he had been enjoying the use of my civvies in my absence. Now it seemed that he would have to buy some new clothes for a change. Should he read this, I am absolutely certain of the fact that he will not even have the grace to blush! This must have been the situation in so many homes during National Service days in Britain. But that was soon to change in our house — sorry Brian!

My bicycle would be a valuable asset to me, it was still in good repair, and in the fifties, the main mode of transport for travelling to and from work.

CIVVY STREET, A NEW JOB AND MARRIAGE

On my arrival home, and after a short break, my priority had to be looking for work. The law stated that the company that any individual had left to do his National Service, were obliged to re-employ that person for at least six months upon his return to civvy street. My first port of call should have been Lake Road Labour Exchange, but I had decided to visit my old governor. In my naivety, I somehow imagined that my old job would be there waiting for me. It started off OK, we shook hands, he said that it was nice to see me and all the other preliminary niceties, and then came the leading question — was I on leave?

"The reason that I am here Mr Tilley, is to start work as soon as possible" I said.

"Well, things are a bit sticky at the moment, I am very short of work and taking anybody on at the moment is really out of the question" he replied. He carried on talking and I believe that he was fully aware of his legal obligations towards me. "Would you be prepared to wait until things pick up? At least you will have your dole money" he said.

Knowing the building trade and the uneven way in which it functioned regarding employment, I knew that that kind of promise was not even worth considering. At this time I had no knowledge whatsoever of the laws regarding re-employment of ex-National Servicemen. So it was thanks, but no thanks! I left the office of Mr Tilley realising that I was back in the real world of civvy street. Of course my father, after listening to my tale, knew instantly what my next course of action should be. Report all the facts to the Labour Exchange and your ex-boss will be summoned to appear before a tribunal. He must employ you for six months. In fact a friend of mine did take this action for the very reason that I have

75

just described, and won hands down. That was the law and it was enforced. Loss of earnings and other items of payment were awarded in his favour. There was very little to be gained by me being on the dole, so I began the search for work. Winning my case for being re-employed by my ex-boss would have been a kind of hollow victory for me. Had I returned to his employ, I firmly believe that the working atmosphere would have been intolerable.

My father suggested that I return to the RAF, which is a course of action that I could have taken with success, but like the fool that I was, I never even considered the possibility of my returning to the Service. In my kind of situation, you are tempted into the trap of accepting almost any offer of work, knowing full well that it is not what you are looking for in conditions and wages, etc.

Good fortune came my way in the shape of a message from my sister Kathleen. It was an instruction to attend an interview with E and A Sprigings Builders; their office being at Highland Road in Eastney. I had never heard of this company, but I really did have good feelings regarding my prospects of work, for reasons that I am unable to explain. My brother-in-law had dealings with this company, and had made enquiries on my behalf regarding employment as a painter, hence the interview. So once more, it is not what you know, it is who you know. The interview went well up to a point. I could have the job, providing that I was willing to work for three pence per hour below the trade rate, for a three-month period. Roger Sprigings and the painter foreman Ted Locke, were asking the questions. Should I make the grade, a place for me on the permanent staff was assured. With an offer like that, who is going to worry about the loss of three pence per hour for three months? The thought of working alongside someone who was earning more for doing the same work, I never had any problems with. The prize would be being made a member of the permanent staff.

The building trade was notorious for employing people on a short-term basis, so it was up to me to prove to my employers that I would be worth keeping in the long term, and this I was able to do, mainly with the help of a new-found friend Ken Toone. Sprigings were a well-established building firm in Portsmouth, and had been operating for many years, and they were noted for their quality of work. MOD contracts and corporation contracts were often tendered for and often won, which was always good news for the workforce of about fifty people. My prospects, or should I say our prospects, were looking good.

My fiancée was employed by the Portsmouth Co-operative Society in the Garnier Street bakery; her first job on leaving school. Her place of work was a five-minute walk from her home in Netley Street. Our immediate goal was to save for our forthcoming marriage, and we did manage to do this, as well as having a fairly full social life. As a matter of interest for some readers, maybe ex-Co-op employees, my future wife's foreman at the bakery was a happy little man called Fred Leggat.

Oddly enough, my very first job in civvy street was to assist another employee in Lake Road Labour Exchange. I had been a regular visitor to this building in the past three weeks seeking employment. My job was to assist another painter replace a rather large piece of glass, and I was ready and waiting at the time stated. The man that I had to assist had already been working in the building, so he of course would be directing operations. This was a good situation as far as I was concerned. I needed time to adjust after three years away from the trade. After an anxious wait, a man came into view somehow managing to push his bicycle loaded with a large piece of glass, putty and his bag of tools. Did someone mention health and safety at work? Not having any idea of what my new workmate looked like, and expecting one of Sprigings' lorries, I made no attempt to go to the assistance of the man pushing the bicycle. You have guessed right, of course the poor sod who was struggling with his loaded bike, was the very man that I was waiting for. He must have thought that he would be working with a right prat; and who could blame him!? This was my first meeting with Ken Toone; a very lucky day for me, as he was a genuinely nice person and, as I was soon to realise, a first-class tradesman. We have been friends ever since that first meeting of nearly fifty years ago.

One of the contracts in which Sprigings were involved, was building a warehouse for Pink and Son in Surrey Street. As all you Pomponians will know, Pinks were a prominent grocer in the city at this time. My orders were to report to the site foreman the following day, a man named Bill Jackson. "What do you want?" were the first words spoken to me by the man in charge. My first thoughts at this greeting were 'Oh bloody hell, I'm in for a rough ride here', but I need not have worried in the slightest. This was Bill's way of breaking the ice, and everyone had the same treatment. It was his way, take it or leave it. At the risk of being a bore and repeating myself, I will say once again that it was my good fortune to meet yet another person who it was a pleasure to work with, and a pleasure to know. That was in 1954, and even though we ceased working together many years ago, I still visit him and his wife Mary at their home in Eastern Avenue.

Having been away from ladder work and working off of scaffolding for three years, as well as gaining a stone in weight, I found the first few days to be very tiring. But I was really happy and looking forward to getting back to the routine of pre-Service days. Tea and lunch breaks in the tommy hut were a real education, with the general conversation and cheerful banter, some of it inevitably ribald that I won't go into here. It was on this site that I would get to know many of the men that I would be working with for the next six years, and it would be my pleasure to do so.

The added bonus of being a civilian once more, was being able to spend so much more time with my beloved June. The sheer pleasure of this though, did not deter me from still enjoying my association with Kangaroo Sports, and a good many of my old associates, like me, had now returned from National Service. The club had had a name change in my absence, and it was now called Argosy; playing in local leagues under that name. Our football meetings were being held at 2 Burlington Road. This was the house of Mr and Mrs Alf Rook, a grand couple of people, giving their time for the youth of Portsmouth.

Having completed my stint of work at Surrey Street warehouse site, it was time to move on to Curzon Howe Road in Portsea. Work here consisted of the complete decoration of all the house exteriors, front and rear, both sides of the road. I must add that it was not before time. I am fairly certain that these houses had not been decorated for ten years.

As I have written, Sprigings were noted for their quality of work. The specification for this work was as follows; Burn off all woodwork, prime, apply two undercoats and one gloss finish. Everyday a corporation clerk of works would be on site, to check progress and quality of work; no skimping here! Ken Toone stuck his neck out for me, when he recommended to the governor that I be paid the full hourly rate of pay; he considered that I was worth it, in view of the fact that casual workers had been taken on, and were being paid the full rate, but they were turning out work that had to be continually checked. Also, at times, they were found to be below the standard required. In view of this, and my general attitude to the job, etc., my raise in pay was agreed; three old pennies per hour. By today's standards I suppose that that sounds a piffling amount of money, but it put another fifteen shillings per week in my pay packet, and added to this, it gave me the feeling that I was being paid the correct rate for the quality of work that I was producing.

To complete my story of working in Curzon Howe Road, it would be very remiss of me not to say a very big thank you to all of those kind people, in fact the majority of the residents, who were kind enough to take the time and trouble, not forgetting the expense, to provide tea, coffee, and very often cold drinks for any painter working on or near their houses. The welcome received from these people made the working day so much nicer. Thanks a lot you Portsea mudlarks!

Hands up those of you working in the building trade, who can honestly say that they have never earned extra money by moonlighting. Very few I would say. My hands stay down. I plead guilty of course. The idea of working is to make as good a living that is humanly possible out of your labour and commitment. But at certain times of the year (mainly wintertime), many building trade workers were prevented from doing so. I will explain this statement by describing the anomalies that have existed in the building trade for many years. Being paid 'wet time'; the criteria being to remain on site for the complete day, eight or nine hours, in other words raining or not raining. You had to be available to work. A full week of this situation (it often happened), would mean losing a third of your week's wages. A standard practice throughout the industry, was being asked to take your holidays whilst the company were hoping for a contract to materialise, but holiday pay never equalled a full working week's pay, so you lose again! Can you imagine the feelings of the men when they were told (not asked) to take a cut in wages every winter? This archaic system existed in the building industry for many years. Six weeks before Christmas, and six weeks after Christmas, short-time working was compulsory; in effect three months in every year. Every man was being forced to take a pay cut, just when a family man needed the money most of all. Is it any wonder then that many tradesmen jumped at the chance of readdressing the balance by moonlighting? Many of the company directors were Freemasons, and I am sure that being a member of this secret society gained you a distinct advantage over the ordinary working man. Without a doubt, employers would never agree with what I have written, but they can hardly deny that many thousands of pounds have remained in their coffers every year, thanks to compulsory short-time working. Moonlighting was never the one-sided evil that many would have us believe. In my fifty years working in the building industry, I never met anyone who enjoyed the prospect of being away from his home for fifteen hours a day to earn a living.

MARRIAGE AND PARENTHOOD

Becoming engaged to be married, is a very meaningful commitment. June and I were very aware of this fact and conducted ourselves accordingly, with complete honesty regarding our finances and talking over every stage of the procedure as we moved toward our wedding day. The date chosen was the 5th March 1955. We decided on this date for two reasons; the first and very important, was the fact that this date suited everyone from both families; secondly, and also very important, was that an income tax rebate would be coming our way, just when we would need it most.

We both saved very religiously for our big day, and still managed to enjoy a fairly full social life. At this time in Portsmouth, there were opportunities for an evening's entertainment with over twenty cinemas to choose from, who each had a programme change twice a week. Many small-time dances (hops) took place on Friday and Saturday evenings, and top-class broadcasting orchestras could be danced to at the Savoy and often at the South Parade Pier. Also trade's clubs and company social clubs could be visited. A lot more could be written on this subject, but I am very sure that it will make the younger reader very envious. I will say that I do feel very sorry for the young people of today's world, trying to make their way along life's rocky road. Just a little example of today's rip-off culture, being charged to walk into a pub because it happens to be New Year's Eve, and maybe the biggest rip-off is the fifteen pounds charged to watch Pompey struggle to put two passes together.

After many hours of wedding talk, by this I mean the usual choosing of bridesmaids, guest lists, venue and very many more arrangements and details to make sure the day would be made to be as near perfect as possible, we would be married in St Mary's Church at 3 p.m., on March 5th 1955. Our reception was to be held in the upstairs hall of the Crystal Palace public house, located on the corner of Fawcett Road and Goldsmith Avenue (now demolished). After the photographs were taken, it was off to the reception venue. June and I were the first to arrive, but oh calamity, the door was locked and it had began to snow heavily. It seemed ages before we gained entry into the pub, but in actual fact inside a few minutes everything was sorted out and we were in the warmth of the hall. To say the whole day was wonderful would be an understatement. We will never be able to thank June's parents enough for the selfless manner in which they made our day so perfect.

Just prior to my wedding, I had been instructed to commence decorating empty premises on the corner of Arundel Street and Guildford Street; a little shop. Nothing unusual about that, I hear you say, but I will explain. By a strange quirk of fate, that little shop is the one that I have already written about earlier on in this narrative. The very shop where my friends and yours truly, as children, pinched so many farthing chews, sherbet dabs and gobstoppers, etc., from the front of the counter. The dear old lady who owned the shop, Miss Coles, met a tragic end. She was burned very seriously and died of her injuries in the Royal Hospital. Suffering from severe arthritis, she was unable to escape when her furniture caught fire in her sitting room at the rear of her shop. I well remember her in the thirties disappearing out the back, to return carrying her cup of tea to drink whilst working, serving her customers. A very sad end to a hard-working old lady.

The company for whom I worked were joint owners of the property, and of course the fire damage had to be repaired and the whole of the premises redecorated, prior to selling. It seems very ironic that Miss Coles was to die in this way. She had opened her shop all through the war years, and somehow survived the bombing and fire all around her, in an area that was severely bombed. Perhaps you will agree with me when I say that fate can be very unfair at times. Talking of fate, here I was employed to decorate the very shop where, as a child, I did most of my petty pilfering.

Like all good grooms I had to have a stag night, and more by good luck than judgement, the night had been arranged two days prior to the wedding, as opposed to the normal one day. My old chums from way back would be my companions for this happy pub crawl. Vic and Ray Spry, John Potter, Reg and Morry Stares and Ken Atkins made up the main core. We met in the Spread Eagle, on to the Lamb and Flag, the Dew Drop Inn and the Bridge Tavern. After that I have no idea! To say that the following morning that I was under the weather, would be an understatement. An almighty hangover, the like of which I had never had before or since, was my punishment for downing too much beer. Unfortunately I held the keys to the shop, so it was imperative that I turn up. After struggling from my bed with a 'serves you right' from my mother ringing in my ears, my plan was to walk from Milton Road to Guildford Street in the hope that it would clear my aching head, and maybe get rid of this horrible feeling of biliousness. Somehow in my clouded mind, I gave thanks that this day was the day prior to my wedding day, and next week I would be on honeymoon. The walk to the shop improved my feeling of wellbeing only very slightly, but on opening the door and walking in, the smell of fresh paint instantly affected my stomach. At once I had to make my way to the kitchen sink. I will leave the rest to your imagination. It was just impossible for me to contemplate working. Now the question of the keys. Vic Spry's family, as I have written, lived in Guildford Street, and Mrs Spry very kindly agreed, as I felt sure that she would, to hold the keys for me. A note on the shop door gave instructions where they were to be found. It was goodbye work for a little while at least. My route home took me through Netley Street; my future wife's house number was twenty. Knowing that she would be home, I decided to call in. June's mother noticed at once that I needed some kind of pick-me-up. "Sit down and I will make you coffee" said Lil. That just about sums up the attitude and helpfulness of Lily Bundy. No recriminations, just concern for others.

We really had gone posh for our honeymoon. One week's bed and breakfast had been booked at the Premier Hotel, Russell Square, London. The bill for our week's bed and breakfast came to thirty-five pounds and we still have the receipt. In 1955 the cost of our week's stay represented six weeks' wages. After paying the hotel bill, we were left with seven pounds and our rail fare. Most of the time whilst staying in London, we were having our meals and snacks in Lyons Corner Houses, and damn good fare it was, at a very reasonable cost. The hotel, admittedly, was really an extravagance we could hardly afford, but never regretted.

My dear wife's wedding ring cost seven pounds and ten shillings; we still have the original receipt from Pickets and Pursers in Commercial Road. Prior to our wedding, my wife ceased working for the Co-op bakery and had taken up a more lucrative position working for Fireproof Tanks at their factory in Dundas Lane. After our honeymoon, June and I returned to 20 Netley Street; my new home. People say, and I have heard it many times, that living with in-laws does not work out. In some cases this is probably correct, however, living with June's mother and father caused us no problems, and I was treated as one of their own. So another thank you to Lily and Arthur!

Soon after our marriage, a post as a cleaner was on offer at C & A in Commercial Road, and as this was within easy walking distance from our home, it would cancel out waiting around for buses travelling to and from Fireproof Tanks; also the wages on offer were almost the same. After an interview, June's application was accepted; the first piece of luck in our married life. On commencing work June was introduced to her supervisor, Mrs Fisher. It is a strange fact in life that you tend to make contact with some families more so than others. George Fisher, the supervisor's son, was a friend of mine. Later on in this story you will learn of my meeting with her other son, Bernard; we were to work together for many years.

If I were asked to nominate an outstanding event in my life, the news that we were to have an addition to our family, in the not too distant future, would take first place. Our first son's predicted birth date was in November. Both families greeted the news with great pleasure, and that added to our happiness. The time came near, and my dear wife was admitted to St Mary's Hospital. Giving birth to my son proved to be very difficult for June, but she came through the ordeal wonderfully well. These are just words written by a man, what would I know of the pain and agony of giving birth? November 3rd 1956, our son Gary Michael was born. June's mother and father could hardly wait for the arrival home of their daughter with their first grandchild. From the very beginning, I could see that my wife had the natural instincts of a loving and caring mother. Not that I ever had any doubts that that was how it would be.

In view of the fact that our family had now become three, we had decided to look for other accommodation. We now needed the extra room. Also we had no wish to impose on Lily and Arthur any further. Of course they never saw the situation as June and I did, but the time had arrived for us to move on and not be dependant on others. The arrival of Gary brought nothing but joy to June's parents and you could almost see the love flowing for our son.

As sometimes happens, luck was to come our way during a search for a house. No.25 St John's Road was available for a rental of one pound per week. The property was badly in need of minor repairs and decorating, but yours truly, being in the trade, saw this as a minor problem. The fact that our new-found house was only five minutes away from Netley Street pleased our parents. Our only toilet was located at the bottom of the garden, and this little building provided living quarters for some really big spiders! For the area, the house was quite spacious; three bedrooms and three small rooms on the ground floor; a scullery, that had only the bare essentials, a gas cooker, cold water tap over a butler sink and wooden draining board, a type of Welsh dresser, two storage cupboards, a table and four chairs — very sparse indeed! Open fires could be used in every room, and please believe me when I say that they were sorely needed. The heat just disappeared into the long passages, upstairs and down, and up into the great stairwell. This was our first house and we were both prepared to work very hard to make it comfortable. You will have noticed that I have not written about, or described, a bathroom. Like so many houses in Portsmouth, and no doubt in England, at the time, a bathroom was unheard of. A bungalow bath was used, which had to be filled with water which had been heated on the gas cooker, or a gas copper. Quite a performance when taking a bath!

Alternatively a bath could be had if you were prepared to make your way to the Victoria Park public bath houses, and very often, weather permitting, I made use of this public amenity. Normally you would have to wait in a queue for a bath cubicle to become vacant. A chair was provided in the cubicle and a wooden deckboard to stand on. This was essential as the floor was concrete with no covering. An attendant in charge allocated cubicles as they became empty. Soap and a towel could be hired, but I always preferred to supply my own. Time for wallowing in your bath was never allowed. The attendant gave you the allotted time (whatever that was), and then hammered on the door, telling you at the same time to make way for others. What I have written is the absolute truth in describing bath time for many people in Portsmouth in the fifties.

I firmly believe that the real test in marriage comes with the arrival of children, especially your first child. The baby must come first in all considerations. Feeding times, changing nappy times, going out times and coping with those sleepless nights, which I will not even try to describe! June had ceased working at C & A with the arrival of our son. My wife was old-fashioned enough to want to be with her baby in his vital years. Being a permanent member of staff at Sprigings, I was enjoying a regular income. Of course we were to notice the difference in losing June's income, and this would be the start of moonlighting in my working life.

A FIRE AND BAD NEWS

E & A Sprigings owned many properties in Portsmouth. They owned houses in Newcomen Road, Winstanley Road, Twyford Avenue, Ranelegh Road and many others in Stamshaw. Many of the tenants were elderly people, coming to the end of their life span. Consequently the houses became empty on a regular basis. It was rare for the houses to be re-let; the usual procedure was for the painters to move in, and spend as little time as possible redecorating the property prior to selling. Working in these dismal houses in wintertime was never very pleasant, more often than not they were without heating, electric light or gas. To warm ourselves, or as a means of making tea, we made a fire with any old timber that we could find. Thank God for open fireplaces. But doing this work was by far a lot better than having no work at all. The painters took it for granted that the lack of contract decorating was due entirely to the season of the year, but we were to learn differently very soon.

It was on a Thursday, late in November. Myself and two other painters were working in a house in Newcomen Road. The only light that we had in the house after 3.30 p.m., was candlelight. Our paypackets were normally brought to us on site on a Thursday. Just picture the scene; we had to wait for our pay to be delivered, and by this time we were an hour beyond our knocking-off time; it was 4.30 p.m., and quite dark. The three of us were waiting in the front room of the house, by candlelight, wondering what had happened to our pay. Eventually Arthur Sprigings, one of the partners, arrived with our money. He apologized at once, saying that he had been held up in a serious traffic jam in Commercial Road, caused by a fire at a corset factory in Regent Street. The factory was actually burnt right out with only a shell remaining.

The real news was yet to come. He went on, "I have some important news for you all, and I am afraid it is not very good. Our company has ceased trading."

I would like you to try and picture the scene in your mind. The four of us standing in a room lit by candlelight, which was casting our shadows to make us look like ogres. This was surely the perfect Dickensian setting or tableau; Mr Bumble telling his servants that they were out of a job, just before Christmas.

There was a glimmer of hope though, because Privett, another building company, had agreed to complete any outstanding contracts, and they were willing to employ a certain number of Sprigings' tradesmen. If I was one of the lucky ones, this would at least carry me over the winter period, including Christmas. We were given no reason for this turn of events, not entirely unexpected of course. I had no choice other than agree to be employed by Privetts, given the opportunity. It was rumoured in the trade that the sudden demise of Sprigings was caused by certain members of the family having their fingers in the till. Not an unheard of situation. I could name other companies in Portsmouth where this did happen. A case of 'Never mind you, Jack. My snout's in the trough'.

Although this was a black time for me, I tried not to let the situation effect my wife, by remaining as happy as possible. The offer of employment by Privetts did come my way. After working a week's notice, it was time to say cheerio to some good workmates, and on the following Monday report to Privetts' offices and workshops on the corner of Stubbington Avenue and Copnor Road, at 7.30 a.m. Needless to say the contracts' manager never reported for work until 9.00 a.m.; what's new?

From the very beginning of starting my new job, I was like a fish out of water. There were one or two telltales, and two brothers who were in a position of authority I found particularly difficult to get along with. Many of the Sprigings' employees who were taken on by Privetts left within a comparatively short period of time, and so, maybe, it seems that I was not the only one to feel disillusioned with the working methods of Privetts. But praise be, I was about to be rescued. My old pal Ken Toone, who had been working for the Co-op building department for about four years, had let me know of a vacancy for a painter and decorator. Well, I was so pleased that I was very tempted to kiss him, but he is so bloody ugly that I abandoned the idea!

An appointment was arranged at Flathouse Road, to meet the foreman painter estimator Len Spratt; one of the gentlemen of this world. My interview went very successfully. My work record of thirteen years since leaving school was faultless, and after discussing the type of work that I would be required to do, and my willingness to work overtime and nightshift, he informed me there and then, that he would like me to commence work as soon as possible. You notice, dear reader, no pussy-footing about with some bimbo from personnel. My interviewer was a tradesman and therefore knew pretty much what he was talking about, and not employed just to make up the numbers in the office! Nothing was to give me more pleasure than to hand in my week's notice to Privetts' building manager. He was a bit surprised and informed me that I was the fifth ex-employee of Sprigings to hand in his notice in a week.

My place of work at this time, was in the old chapel or church in Edinburgh Road, just by the level crossing, which was to be temporary work premises for Twilfits, whose factory had burned to the ground in Regent's Street, back in November. One more week of working for a company that I disliked, then I would be back working with my old pal Ken Toone on the Co-op building department!

TWO WISE MOVES AND FAMILY CELEBRATIONS

One other painter had been taken on, and his starting day coincided with mine, and from that time Berny Fisher and I were to work together for twenty years — another lucky period in my life. Working conditions in the Co-op building department were second to none. All union rules and conditions were followed, and a high standard of workmanship was always maintained, both on Co-op properties and customer work. The Co-op board of directors at this time, with Mr Wynne in the chair when meeting the departments' representatives, were always good listeners and fair negotiators, which in turn will always produce a happy workforce. How unfortunate that this good relationship was to change so drastically, caused by a couple of rotten apples in the barrel, whom I believe had their brains exchanged for degrees! More of this part of my story later.

This was a happy time for June and I. A new position for me, with a job that I enjoyed and never envisaged leaving, and more happy news on my arrival home from work. "The doctor confirmed it today, Mick. I am pregnant" said June. June had always said that she would like two children, and I will make no secret of the fact that I was hoping that our next child would be a girl. Both sides of the family, once again, were very pleased on hearing our good news. The thing that has always amazed me is my wife's ability to always take things in her stride, and cope with whatever situation arises, good or bad. During her nine-month pregnancy the housework and looking after her family was always to the fore. I am truly a lucky man.

The time had arrived for our baby to be born, and who was there to give marvellous assistance? It was Lily of course; her mum. Our second child was born on 11th March 1960 at 25 St John's Road, Landport. He was christened David John in St Faith's

Church, Crasswell Street. Yet another male born into the Franckeiss lineage. The latest of a very long line of males traced back to 1600.

My wife was to recover very quickly from her confinement, and it did my heart good to observe the wonderful way that she cared for our two little boys.

Just a little more about the advantages of working for the Co-op building department. As an employee the use of the social club was granted automatically. It was a really great place to take our family for the evening. The full title of the club was as follows: Employees' Welfare Association (EWA). Many functions were on offer throughout the year if any employee with guests wished to take part. My congratulations to a very fine club committee. If you were a family man, then a function that was never missed were the children's Christmas parties. A very special mention here for Alf Morton, head buyer and storeman at Flathouse building department. He worked extremely hard to make these kids' parties so successful. Not only did he do this for his own department, but for all employees' children of Portsea Island Co-op. Thanks so much Alf for the happiness that you brought to our children, year after year.

Co-op works' department darts team; Co-op Social Club; Standing, left to right, Rob, me, Mick Gee, Tony Goldring, Alan Doney, Ray Street. Sitting, Ron Fleet, Sean Coghlin, Bob Vining — good days!!

91

How many of you tried in vain to obtain tickets for the Co-op Christmas or summer dances? The normal venue being South Parade Pier. No time was to be lost when the tickets became available, as the events were so popular, particularly the New Year's Eve knees-up. Shame on me; I had applied too late for tickets. But all was not lost. Taffy Davis, an employee of the works' department and also a volunteer doorman for this dance, was my saviour. A quick bung of a quid or two and my problem was solved; a good honest fiddle.

The problem never arose of getting home after midnight, as the Corporation Transport Department laid on many buses to all districts for a one-shilling standard fare. Real buses with a conductor who actually smiled at you! How things have changed in Pompey.

Whilst touching on the subject of public transport, I will go on further to say that what a pleasure it was to be able to use the Southdown buses for travelling to and from work, confident in the knowledge that they would almost, without fail, be on time. Also there were happy times when my family and I took a train ride when it was still called British Rail. My wife's father was employed as a purser on the Isle of Wight ferries, and was allowed privileged tickets for his family. What a treat it was to go aboard the paddle steamer, on a trip up to Southampton Water to see the ocean-going liners. June's mother had been a waitress on the paddle steamers in 1929. We still have a photograph of her taken at this time in her uniform, and what a great picture it is! I very much doubt if there would be room for a cup and saucer in the rust buckets that are used today for the crossing to the island; certainly no room for a waitress.

June and I had decided that now was a good time as any to look for a suitable property to buy. The fact that I looked to have a secure future working for the Portsea Island Co-operative Society, to give it its full name, prompted this decision. The challenge now was to find a property that suited our requirements and our present financial position. Challenge is the right term. Building societies were not as free with their mortgage lending in 1960 as they are today. The rule was that a mortgage was granted according to your means, and this rule was strictly adhered to. If you were earning a fairly low wage, as I was at this time, then the property was chosen accordingly. After a great deal of searching, a property that we were invited to inspect in Fifth Street seemed to meet our every requirement. Not a luxurious house by any standard. On the plus side it had a bathroom as well as an indoor toilet, and to June and I this was a real plus and probably a deciding factor in our considerations. When we actually made up our minds to buy 20 Fifth Street, we had moved up a peg in our living standard. The house did require a considerable amount of work to be done, mainly decorating, to bring it up to tiptop condition. We had agreed to the asking price for this house, which was twelve hundred and fifty pounds. Maybe a younger reader will smile at this seemingly small sum, but to put it into its true context, just let me explain that our outlay for housing, almost at once, would double from one pound per week to two pounds per week, plus maintenance, insurance, rates, and solicitors' fees.

Like many of you, I am sure, after the completion of the business of buying your first house, when one then had time to reflect, you would wonder if you had done the right thing. We were down to our last few pounds. The obvious answer from my point of view was to turn to moonlighting, and this is exactly the course that I took to put money in the bank. I worked fourteen hours a day for long spells, many, many times in my young working life, and very often this included weekends and working overtime when asked to do so by the Co-op. Of course working long hours will cause friction in the household, and I do understand the reasons for this. There are not many men who would rather be working and spending time away from their families. The men that I have known would much rather be at home with the wife and kids. For me marriage was an undertaking to provide for my family, and I was endeavouring to do just that. If housewives are reading this, and at this time spending many hours in the house without their husbands for reasons of work, please try and understand that he is doing his best for the family.

1963 — A MIXED YEAR

It has been said that people remember times and events more by the weather of the time than for any other reason. It is not to prove a point that I will write my memories of the awful winter of 1963. This part of the British Isles, I am happy to write, very rarely experiences winters as bad as the winter of 1963. Here are some facts and figures, and also some first-hand knowledge, from a person who worked from January until the end of May in awful weather; repairing conservatories, guttering and snow guards, leaking roofs and also drying out homes that had been flooded, the cause being burst pipes. Of course every call out was deemed an emergency by the person making the call.

Tradesmen worked in pairs doing this work, and my partner for the five-month period was Ray Spry (brother of Vic). To give you an idea of the workload generated by the freezing weather, the Co-op building department used twenty-five hundredweights of putty for glazing, plumbing and guttering joint repairs; thousands of gutter bolts, snowguard brackets and screws, lengths of guttering and snowguards and thousands of square feet of glass; the list of materials is endless. To put it into perspective, this type of building ware became unobtainable in Portsmouth, and the building department lorries were driven to London to buy as much as possible of this type of material. The Co-op works' department provided a real service in those days! Bricklayers of companies other than the Co-op were laid off. It was just not possible to lay bricks in the freezing weather, as the mortar would turn to ice in seconds. So, once again, unless inside work could be found for the brickies, it would mean a lot of hardship for the men and their families. The majority of the work undertaken at the outset of the big freeze, was through claims on the house insurance. Many,

many times customers were to tell me that the claim that they were making, would be the very first in twenty or thirty years of paying premiums, and I also heard tales of insurance companies refusing to pay their customers storm damage, usually for some nefarious reason. It seems to me that not a lot has changed in the world of insurance.

An event that was to serve me well in the latter part of 1963, was the opening of an hotel almost opposite South Parade Pier. A painter friend of mine was approached by the new owners of this hotel, to get together a gang of painters to work a regular amount of hours 'moonlighting', to decorate rooms, bathrooms, stairwells, passages, in fact the whole of the premises from top to bottom. Some undertaking! This approach was made in October, with a view to open the hotel in the following spring. Interested parties were invited to a meeting at the hotel to talk over details, and most important of all the hourly rate. Each painter was to have his own attendance book, and the hours worked paid for every Friday evening. This was agreed by all the would-be moonlighters. Many other trades were involved, not forgetting Knight & Lees carpet fitters, all after moonlight money. At the height of the work, no less than nineteen painters were working evenings and weekends. I have never known or heard of a decorating job of that nature being completed by part-time work. We earned our money, which mostly paid for the families' Christmases, plus a bit over, but it was no easy skive. The hotel did open, and start trading in the spring. I do know the names of all the painters who took part in this, probably, one-off moonlight bonanza, but I will keep mum.

A number of my family had made the decision to move abroad. John Blake, my uncle whom I mentioned earlier, had had enough of English winters, and had made up his mind to live and work in Australia. Being a bachelor, he was in the happy position of being able to travel where he pleased, and at any time that he pleased. This he did with a caravan and a sole companion, a little black and white terrier, and there he stayed until his death in 1995.

My younger brother Brian and Lucy his wife, also made the decision to try their luck abroad and made Rhodesia their choice of country. We had a farewell party out at Cowplain and I have the feeling that they were more sad than they cared to show. Well I can tell them now, although at the time I never let my feelings show as I put a brave face on it, but inwardly I was feeling very sad. As the saying goes, 'all is well that ends well', because Brian and his family are now home and living in Chichester, and I can only just believe that he has reached the ripe old age of sixty-three. Nearly an old git, like me!

My other brother Terry, who is younger than Brian and I, decided with his wife Jackie, to up sticks and also try their luck in Rhodesia, and after a comparatively short stay, they moved on to Eastern Transvaal in South Africa where Terry worked in the coal mining industry as an electrical supervisor. Sad to say he is not, or never has been, a very good communicator, so we have lost touch. It is very sad for this to happen. I tried very hard to stop this situation continuing, to no avail. He and his family have been in South Africa for nearly forty years. If, or when he does return to Portsmouth, he will see some almighty changes. However, should he decide to return home, I will be the first to shake his hand and say welcome back.

LIFE IS NOT ALL WORK

A regular trip out away from family duties for **June** and I, would be a visit to the cinema. Admission prices at the time were very reasonable, and because of this our trips to the cinema were easily affordable. The people of Portsmouth were really spoilt for choice when deciding which cinema to visit. Taking in the areas of Fareham, Havant, Gosport, Cosham and even Waterlooville, inclusive of Portsmouth, there were over twenty cinemas to choose from. Added to this was the fact that programmes in each cinema were changed twice a week, normally on Sundays and Thursdays. Two films were shown as well as newsreels, and very often a cartoon, all for a couple of bob or less, if you did not mind sitting in the first, second, or third row. June and I would normally visit the cinema on a Sunday afternoon with her sister Pamela and her husband Peter. Local to us, and within easy walking distance, was the Savoy, Plaza, Troxy or the Classic. We really had a wonderful choice of films to watch in those days. Here I will take a little time to thank June's mum and dad for looking after the kids whilst we enjoyed our Sunday afternoons at the pictures.

Television at this time, in the black and white form, was in many people's homes, and the advertising campaign to urge you to buy or rent a colour television had really begun in earnest. People, it seemed, never needed very much persuasion. The fact is if you wanted to rent a colour set from the Co-op, you were placed on a waiting list to await your turn, such was the demand. A colour set was available at once from other companies, but the televisions were of inferior quality, and to say the least, very unreliable. So in the long run it was advisable to wait for the better set from the Co-op. As an employee of the Co-op, and at the time working in Co-op House in Fratton Road (the one-time flagship of the Portsea Island Co-operative Society, since replaced by a posh street market), I knew and was quite friendly with the man who had control of the TV waiting list, and I'm ashamed to say that I tried to coerce this man into moving me up the waiting list a place or two. But I should have known better, he was a man of integrity, and as friendly as we were, would not even consider my suggestion (well done that man). We did eventually receive our colour television set from the Co-op, and only very rarely did it cause us problems.

What a vast difference in comparison to our rent-a-set receiver that my parents had in our home in Milton Road in 1945–1950. It only had three stations, not that I listened to the radio very often, but I did listen to ITMA, The Goons, Workers' Playtime, Wilfred Pickles and Dick Barton. To be truthful I spent very little time indoors. Even so, I know for sure that my parents enjoyed listening to the programmes on the little rent-a-set.

One of the finest assets that a wife could have, is that of being a good and competent manager, and in June Bundy I had married one of the best. Once again 'lady luck' had smiled on me! Having by this time lived in Fifth Street for four years, our financial position allowed us to consider the possibility of buying our first car. June was working part-time in a small shop and therefore putting more money into the kitty. We did our sums and decided that we could afford to buy and run a car. A tricky situation to say the least is one of buying a second-hand car. However our maroon Ford Anglia turned out to be a very good buy. I am sorry to say that, in effect, I was one of the contributors of the demise of those good people of the Portsmouth City Bus service. I regret that very much, but I regret even more the privatised replacement that we have now. An advantage that we did have, of course, was the use of a car whilst our children were young, and the roads were nowhere near as crowded as they are today. Just as a point of interest, the cost of our four-year-old Anglia was two hundred and ninety pounds. To purchase a new Anglia was out of our reach at five hundred pounds.

ANOTHER BUREAUCRATIC BLUNDER

The *Portsmouth News* has been our daily paper since our marriage, and I have been reading the *News* from about the age of twelve. It was in the *News* that we were to learn of the intention of the Portsmouth Planning Department to compulsory purchase our home in Fifth Street to make way for a road. Not a very nice way to learn of something so tremendously important to a man's family, but then again, when have city planners ever taken into consideration the feelings or interests of their citizens? — and, I might add, the very people that allow them to draw such high salaries. To add insult to injury, our mortgage had been granted to us from the City Council, who at the time of granting our mortgage, assured my wife and I that no development whatsoever was envisaged for the Fifth Street area. The lesson here, I believe is never believe a word that a city planner or developer has to say. Has anyone who has had dealings with City Council departments of this nature, ever won the day, and have actually heard heads of departments hold up their hands and admit that they were wrong? It is an impossibility to meet these superdodgers face to face unless of course, one can pay for an army of barristers.

The Council followed their normal procedure of grinding a hard-working family man into the ground with bureaucratic red tape and dogma. Since the occupation of our new home, many hours had been spent making improvements to the property, and a great deal of money had been spent, which I could hardly afford. The chance of recouping this money, where compulsory purchase is involved, is absolutely nil. The owners of the property, in actual fact, are given a few crumbs, and in effect it is take it or leave it; but you must get out. By the end of reckoning, my wife and I would lose no less than four thousand pounds for this Portsmouth

City Council's bureaucratic blunder. A hell of a lot of money for a family to lose.

Up until this point in our marriage, June and I will have made the right decisions concerning our day-to-day lives. There is a grain of comfort to be had knowing that this situation arose through no fault of ours. A mistake, I will admit, is agreeing to move into Council property, although on reflection, it is no surprise after experiencing the stress and trauma of losing your home. Another house to move into would have been very nice, and we did express our desire to do just that, but the 'nice man' from the Council put all kinds of obstacles in our way; mainly that we could not have a house. Reluctantly we agreed to move to a newly-built maisonette in Greetham Street. We were caught on the rebound and had we had more time to consider our situation, and dug our heels in and insisted on a house to rent, we would have avoided the mistake of moving into a maisonette. If it had have been possible from a financial point of view, then to buy another house would have been the sensible thing to do. As it was, renting was the only alternative until we were able to make good our losses from the Council fiasco. Luckily June and I came through this bad patch in our lives without any ill effects. We were determined to look to the future, and June had very good reason to do so! I had a husband type feeling that she was keeping something from me.

GOOD NEWS AND TWO SAD EVENTS

After the upheaval and the awful experience of Fifth Street, we both imagined that it would take a long time for us to become settled in our new home, but surprisingly we seemed to get back into our routine very quickly. It helped a great deal, from my point of view, that I was very happy in my job, and I was convinced of the fact that I would work for the Co-op until my retirement. This situation gives a feeling of wellbeing, a happy state that politicians and employers never seem, or want to understand.

Is it a fact that women are full of surprises? Of course it is. In this respect June was no different to the rest of the 'sisterhood'. "Mick, would you mind if I had another baby?" It is not the kind of question that I could answer at once, but it never really mattered. June had had it confirmed that another baby was on the way. My first question after the initial shock wave had passed, was "How do you feel about the situation, with the prospects of so much more hard work ahead of you?" The answer was no more or less than I expected, as June was not in the least bit worried. My dear wife was a natural when it came to caring for babies, as she had already demonstrated with Gary and David. Should our new baby arrive at the expected time, it would mean the difference of ten years from our last born. An expectant father is never obliged to break the news to his workmates, but I had no compunction about doing so, fully expecting to hear all kinds of ribald comments, and I was not disappointed. Being thirty-seven years of age, I suppose 'You randy old git' was appropriate. Ron Fleet's words, "What colour is the milkman's hair?" From Bern Fisher, "You ought to work harder, then you wouldn't have the energy for these high jinks." They were some of the nicer comments. There was never any question of my taking any offence. It never troubled me one bit, after all this is what I consider workmates are for. It would have hurt me more if they had not said these things. Secretly I hoped that our next child would be a girl. At least I imagined that my thoughts were a secret, but I had forgotten that women could read men's minds through a lead shield. Knowing full well that I wished for a little daughter, I was asked by June not to make up my mind that this would be the case. This was my wife's way of letting me down gently before the event. As usual with this lady always considering other people's feelings.

Two o'clock on a February morning, and I had just been summoned to St Mary's Hospital maternity ward. It was snowing, but my thoughts were concentrated on my destination, not the weather. Making my way to the ward, I was asking myself the question "Boy or girl? Boy or girl?" The baby was brought out to me in a little cot by an Australian doctor. "You have a baby son, Mr Franckeiss, and I am sad to say that he has been born with a hair lip."

As the doctor was very quietly breaking the news to me, I was looking at my dear little boy. As any parent will know when looking at your newborn child for the first time, there is a wonderful feeling of love that seems to well up inside you. My heart went out to this poor little mite, only hours old and disfigured. The doctor did a marvellous job of reassuring me that all would be put right, and urged me to go to my wife. If June was disappointed in any way then she never let it show, such is the strength and character of this lady. "It's another boy, Mick, and don't worry we will soon have him right." I think for me this was the most emotional experience of my life. My wife had just been through a very painful confinement, and she was doing her best to reassure me!

Our son was born on the 17th February 1970. He was christened Glen Arthur; Arthur being his grandfather's name. After a series of operations at Odstock Plastic Surgery Hospital; the first at the age of three months, our son came through with flying colours. The operations were performed by Mr Laing, a truly great man and master surgeon. He proved that Aussie doctor right, as it did all work out fine and we can never thank him enough. Sad to relate though, is the fact that that fine surgeon was to die of a brain tumour at the age of fifty-seven. This is certainly not a just world; a man who has done so much for mankind, taken at such a young age. Odstock Hospital, near Salisbury, now has a Laing Ward in memory of a fine man.

When writing of events in your life, it is a temptation to leave out the events that make for sad reading, but to relate a true story, and this story is true, sad happenings must also be recorded. Prior to our third son being born, my father-in-law, Arthur, had become very ill and admitted to the Royal Hospital. The dreadful news was that he was ill with cancer. Arthur was only sixty years old, and I had convinced myself that he would get better and return home. I continued working and had made arrangements to return home immediately, should I be required to do so. Roger Badnell and I were working together, painting the outside of a bungalow in Drayton. The owner had kindly agreed to take any telephone calls on my behalf. Whilst moving to another quarter of the bungalow, I noticed a blackbird on the lawn and I stopped at once, just to observe. The bird never moved. I cautiously gathered the bird into my hands and found that his heart was only just beating. I love all wildlife and I was saddened to see this little bird in distress. After a period of about fifteen minutes, the bird stopped breathing. At the same time the lady of the house called me to the telephone. My wife had telephoned me to give me the news of her father's death. Believe me when I say that I do not believe in ghosts or the supernatural, but I do wonder if this happening was just coincidence or something else. Perhaps you could tell me?

Arthur died in June 1969, a very sad time for the whole family. I have already praised Arthur for the man he was. If I could be half the man that he was, I would be very happy. British Rail very kindly agreed to lay on a ferry for the family to have his ashes scattered on the Solent Water, where Arthur had spent so many hours of his working life as a purser; very often aboard the paddle boats and the modern ferries introduced in the fifties and later pushed out of service; a retrograde step in my humble opinion. After coming off a twelve-hour shift, particularly in the summer season, Arthur and his wife would walk round to the Dial public house in Crasswell Street for a nice cool glass of beer or two. We all have nice memories of a very nice man.

Many of you, I feel sure, will remember the four-day working week that was to hit the country in the mid-seventies. This situation was to affect many people in their working and domestic lives. As I have written, everybody would be involved. Many companies had to act very quickly to continue trading during this period, to avoid a very serious financial loss. The Co-op, my employer, leaned very heavily on their building department to help them through this difficult period. Just to explain the reason for a four-day working week. It was a system devised to enable the Government to ration power, electricity and gas. Some of the workforce throughout the country were to suffer financially during this horrible period of industrial strife. But credit where it is deserved. No loss of wages was incurred by any Co-op employee at this time.

Working for customers provided a wonderful amount of work for the building department, even without advertising, I might add. The works had a wonderful reputation, earned mainly by the highly-skilled tradesmen. My customer at this time, a lady, had contacted the Co-op for the decoration of her staircase, and in my experience any woman that has made up her mind to have decorating carried out in her home, will never be deterred. This lady had agreed to pay extra money for weekend working to avoid the power rationing.

Petrol rationing was about to be introduced, with petrol coupons issued to people relying on their vehicles for work purposes. A big percentage of the tradesmen were owners of cars and many of them, especially those employed on customer work, used their cars for collecting materials from Flathouse and transporting them to their place of work. Also the same system was used when buying from builders' merchants. The correct procedure was to telephone your order to Flathouse and await delivery. Such was the amount of work and lack of works' vehicles that this system had all but collapsed. The alternative was to wait for delivery; a disaster for estimated work. The use of private cars was of course known by the department managers, but never recognised, therefore no recompense for running costs were ever made. You might think 'Why not refuse to use your own cars?' Such was the calibre of the men that the first consideration was for the customer. I think it is called being conscientious. Two men within responsible positions in the department, were aware of the situation regarding the use of private cars, and were forced to use other devious methods of rewarding our loyalty, and I might add, all perfectly legal.

Emergency generators had to be purchased and installed in all the Co-op retail outlets and many other workplaces, as an alternative means of electricity. The work of setting up these machines had to be taken on by the departments' electricians, and at the same time carry on with their normal workload. It was really a busy time for the departments' tradesmen. The electricians were actually seen to be working!! Now there is a one-off (what an awful thing to say)! The storm was weathered and compared with other companies, the Co-op fared reasonably well in very difficult conditions.

My dear father had been taken ill and confined to his bed. His health had been deteriorating over the past year, and he should have been admitted to hospital, but my mother preferred to nurse him at their home in Burgate Close in Leigh Park. I am fairly certain that my mother had a very strong feeling that he was about to die, and she wanted to be by his side until the very end. After suffering a great deal of pain, he passed away on the 16th October 1974. My memories of him will be memories of a kind man, and a man who very rarely lost his temper. Us kids gave him plenty of reasons for losing his temper, and when it did it would be the threat of a clip round the ear, but only a threat; never did my father strike any of his family. His life was never easy. In fact like many people of his time, he must have found life very difficult. As a young man he had to live with the fact that his mother was an alcoholic, and I believe that seeing his mother in a drunken state on so many occasions gave him good reason to keep out of public houses, and he did. A pint of beer was never his tipple, it was always half a pint of light ale to be taken at home, and on only special family events. My father was a gentleman and I will always remember him as such.

Without doubt, I remember the summer of 1976 as the hottest summer I have experienced. It seemed to go on forever; not the normal English summers — a few days of sunshine interspersed with wind and rain. The sun would be shining when we were on our way to work, and continued shining well into late evening. Whilst doing exterior decorating, I will admit to trying to work in the shade, but it was a real treat to be able to work through and complete an outside job without having to stop because of inclement weather! 1976 was the only summer that I have been swimming late in the evening, and to sit on Eastney Beach at ten o'clock at night eating fish and chips, is almost unheard of.

1976 was also the year of our first journey abroad on holiday. June's school friend and neighbour of the forties and fifties had married Peter Newton, and between them had decided that it would be better for the family to emigrate to Canada. Shirley, Peter and their two children, Janice and Paul, sailed to Canada in the early sixties. June and Shirley corresponded regularly, and after many invitations from Shirley and Peter to pay them a visit, we had finally saved enough money to do so. Flying out from England, we were able to see for ourselves the parched countryside of England. We flew to Vancouver and had a very nice holiday with our old Pomponian friends. For those of you who may want to know Shirley's maiden name, it was Hayles, and she lived in Netley Street.

ANOTHER MOVE AND SACRIFICIAL LAMBS

As nice as the accommodation was in the maisonette, the fact was that it would never be our own property, always played a part in my silent thoughts. Also the fact that it was situated on the first floor made it a bit wearing, having to negotiate two flights of stairs when entering or leaving your home. To be brutally truthful, we both considered that Rednal House was no longer a very nice place to live and bring up a family. Certain members of that little community had decreed that they would run riot and forsake all the rules of decent living. I hear you say that I am a prude. As much as I dislike writing this, the fact is I am telling the truth. The housing department, in their wisdom, decided that mixing so-called problem families with normal living families was curing the problems of these people. Not a bit of it. It was the Council's way of just pushing their problems on to their unfortunate tenants. It seemed fairly obvious that this state of affairs would never be resolved, however much the genuine tenants complained, therefore our only answer was to move on out of this sad environment, and rectify our mistake of renting.

The Government, in conjunction with the Abbey National Building Society, were introducing a scheme for Council tenants to obtain a mortgage. Certain rules were laid down and the criteria to be met was as follows: 'Regular payments of rent to the Council during applicant's tenancy. Annual salary with a letter from the employer confirming same. Also a letter from the Council supporting the application or not.'

After safely negotiating these hurdles, the next step was to find a suitably-priced property. Once again, June and I were house hunting. Mainly because of the price, we were able to buy a house in Frogmore Road in Milton. It was very run down and neglected, but I could see that with a lot of work between us, June and I would make it into a nice home for the family. Admittedly it is not the best of locations, but money governs all things. Realistically it is not a bit of use moving to an area and then grumble about the conditions. However, all that it needed was a little consideration for residents of that area, from the officials of Portsmouth Football Club, and a lot more co-operation from the police, then life would have been more pleasant for everyone.

With a great deal of work and determination, that shambles of a house was turned into a nice comfortable home to be proud of, and a stepping stone to the house that we now own. Perhaps this would be my opportunity to say thank you to the people who gave me valuable help at this time, especially to Alec Gordon, an electrician who did all the re-wiring.

Right out of the blue came rumour and talk of redundancies in the Co-op building department. Everyone hoped that it was only a rumour, and as usual in circumstances such as this, companies do their utmost to stop information reaching the workforce until the very last minute. A certain member of the board did break a few rules, and I was secretly forewarned of impending doom. We took an interest in, and read, the Co-op Annual Report, and it made good reading from the workforce point of view. Our society was going from strength to strength.

At long last, union representatives were summoned to meet Co-op management, and I was one of those reps. The Co-op had already made up their minds to make a big percentage of the building department workforce redundant, but please 'dear workmen' don't make trouble for us; bad publicity and all that, don't you know! The question was asked regarding the future of the department and this was the reply; 'If sixty employees are made redundant immediately, then it would secure the jobs of the remainder.' Where had I heard that before? Of course, these people were lying to us. The decision to close the works' department completely had already been made. In fact, after the initial sackings, it was only a matter of fifteen months and the remainder of the workforce were sacked; approximately one hundred and fifty people; all of them honest, hard-working, conscientious, trustworthy employees. Other departments were to close in a short space of time, like the works' sacrificial lambs on the altar of the hypermarket! What hypermarket, I hear you say? Of course, it is not there any more, is it?

The question will always be asked 'How could a company, famed locally for its fair treatment of its employees, change so dramatically in so short space of time?' I think that I will answer the question by saying that it is not always the company's fault, but the fault of certain persuasive individuals, who somehow make their own opinions override all others, whether they be right or wrong. One of these individuals I could name; the one who did the damage.

It was my privilege to work alongside those Co-op employees, not only from the works' department, but everywhere on the Portsea Island Co-operative Society.

HAPPIER TIMES

Such was the good name of the Co-op building tradesmen, that the manager of Leigh Park Council Services, having heard, or read, of so many good tradesmen being given the sack, had the courtesy and good sense to offer employment with an immediate start. This was good news, as it would mean no loss of earnings whilst looking for work. Priorsdean Crescent was to be my first and last employment for the Leigh Park depot.

Within a few weeks of working, a vacancy was being advertised in the *Portsmouth News* for a painter to work for the South-East Hampshire Health Authority based at Queen Alexandra Hospital in Cosham. The necessary forms were completed, and then came the agonising wait.

A letter arrived requesting me to attend QA Hospital for an interview. Strange to say, but I did feel that I would be successful in landing this job, mainly because of my excellent track record regarding my past employment and experience in the trade. The interview was to take place on G level of the hospital in the works' offices, and I was there in attendance at the appointed time. The two people about to do the interview put me at ease at once. Mr Ian Thorburn, the building manager, had served his time as a carpenter (never mind!!), and it fell to him to ask the pertinent questions. Margo Brown represented the personnel section of the interviewers, and she came over to me as a very knowledgeable lady, on top of her job. A stark contrast from the bimbos of today's personnel. It was a very fair interview overall, but I was very pleased when it concluded with the words heard so many times 'Thank you for attending. We will let you know in due course by letter whether you have been successful.' Oh dear, more waiting.

You must have luck in this world, and my luck came to me on this occasion, in the shape of a letter informing me that I had got the job that I wanted at the hospital. The letter was dated 12.3.1980, and how about this for a job title, and I quote, 'Painter, Northern Sector Periphery, based at Queen Alexandra Hospital, Maintenance Ancillary.' My weekly pay was to be £70.80 with £1.50 bonus; not a great deal of money, but a real good job.

On my day of commencing work, I had to report to the foreman, a Mr Ken Jolley; how is that for a good omen? It is always nice meeting new workmates, and by a strange quirk of fate my chargehand had been working with me as an apprentice at the Co-op. His name is Ray Old, and just to think, I taught him all those skills! Some said that this could be payback time, but there was nothing to pay back. I always got on well with Ray, and I still do.

Another man that I was to meet, I had not seen for many years, and I had no idea that he was employed as a painter at QA. His name was Den Atkins, and we ran the streets of Landport in the 1930s; such is fate!

My first job with the NHS was to be at Cosham Health Centre. Mr Jolley very kindly made a point of putting me to work with Den Atkins, after realising that we were already acquainted; very decent of him, I thought.

The work in the Health Centre was only for a short time, and I was really looking forward to starting work in the main hospital. My first impression was of friendliness from the moment that I entered the ward areas. The domestic ladies invariably greeted you with "I hope you buggers are not going to leave a mess for me to clean up." Any of those special ladies who know me, may by chance be reading this, and will know instantly that I am joking. The situation was always the reverse. Usually came the question "Would you like tea or coffee?" I have lost count of the number of drinks made for me by the domestics. A more cheerful group of workers I have yet to meet; they do a wonderful job of cleaning, but also in my opinion, and this is something that hospital management always seem to miss or ignore, the domestics are a damn good morale booster for the patient. Many of these ladies have forgone part of their lunch hour to do shopping for a patient. Acts of kindness such as this are repeated many times. If only the worth of these people were to be reflected in their pay packets.

Queen Alexandra Hospital works' dept. Retirement of
Doug Old, chippy. A wonderful bunch of workmates.

June, myself and the rest of the family were looking forward, very much, to a date in August; a day that our son Gary, was to marry Sally Hitchcock. Sally was born in Colyton, a village near Seaton in Devon. It was Sally's wish that she could be married in the church at Colyton, where she had been christened. We had no objections whatsoever; we were pleased that she had asked us for our opinion. Of course, this would mean a bit more organisation in arranging for guests travelling, etc., but June and I were happy to fall in with whatever came along. Sally's parents, Kath and Geoff, did a great job with arranging the reception and the thousand and one details that are always a part of a wedding. August came and the day of the wedding; a wonderful day for everyone; a day that June and I will always look back on with great pleasure.

QA HOSPITAL, NEW BROOMS AND ALL THAT

"If it ain't broke, don't mend it." There is a great deal of sense in those words, as you will understand on reading further. About this time I was asked to be union representative for my colleagues in QA building department, dealing with health and safety and working conditions, etc. At the beginning of my appointment to this work, I had the pleasure of working with enlightened members of management. Namely my own manager, Ian Thorburn, foreman Alan Knight, Phil Hawkins and his staff, and John Tuck head of personnel. These people were a joy to work with. The concerns of the workforce, notably health and safety, extra money for working out of cradles a hundred feet above ground level, weekend and night working and many day-to-day problems, would always be discussed in an amicable way, and generally a solution and/or a compromise would be found.

Then came the 'new broom'. This needs to be said, so I will say it. Craftsmen in Portsmouth, and no doubt in many other naval ports, have always been plagued by, usually, ex-naval petty officers who have read it all in a book just prior to being demobilised, and because they are ex-navy and in Portsmouth, they fall into some nice little management job. Very often an interviewer would also be ex-navy and, if this was the case, Jolly Jack would be ninety-five per cent sure of being selected. Even if they were to meet the criteria for the post that they were applying for, which would be unique, then their man management skills, without any doubt, would be absolutely minimal. Any ex-servicemen will know that officers never discussed anything with lower ranks, whatever the nature of the business, it was always "Do as I say, or else". Of course, this was their idea of management in civilian life. Why is it that these bullies always managed to disrupt and destroy a smooth and successfully working operation?

It became my misfortune to have to work with two of these characters, or at least I did try very hard to work with these people. They always seemed to have a problem with craftsmen who invariably knew their jobs inside and out. These so-called managers invariably never had a clue, so they would shout to make up for their own incompetence, as they would have done when in command of some unfortunate sailors. We had come to the end of a pleasant working relationship with management, now it was "Do as I say" followed by the infantile "or I will call in a private contractor." As I have said, "If it ain't broke . . . ."

Now is a good time to write of normal, happy people. Working in any establishment as a maintenance operator, would mean having access to just about every department. People view a hospital mainly as wards, theatres and out-patients, but this is not the complete picture. Whatever the department, and everyone is important, it is the dedicated people that make each department function in a smooth and efficient way. Wherever maintenance was required in QA, nursing staff, office staff, portering and just about everybody, were generally friendly and helpful. The introduction of computers and job tickets at vast expense, tended to make the tradesmen's work more difficult and frustrating. This new system of working, cancelled completely the goodwill and extra help that previously a tradesman was able to give to department heads. "If it is not on the ticket, ignore it," a difficult thing to do for a man who is by nature, normally obliging. But as they say, that is progress.

I will give you a couple of examples to illustrate the co-operation between the maintenance staff and hospital administration. Many office staff at QA work in very cramped conditions. My work had taken me to a very small office on D level. Three desks, all necessary, and all the other office paraphernalia had made this office very cramped indeed. I had a job to do and at the same time the office had to continue to function. The young lady, whose job it was to arrange appointments for consultants, understood this perfectly well and acted accordingly. We both did our work in a happy and friendly manner, and not only did everything run smoothly, but time was found to make me a mug of tea! Many thanks Anna, for some nice memories.

A major alteration to the main X-ray department on C level had to be achieved with the office to remain in operation, made possible of course by a major contribution from the office staff. Perhaps if I mention their names, and give them the praise that they all deserve, the consultants will be moved to have a whip-round and treat all of the office to a slap-up meal! There was Miss Flood, with that Bristol burr; Bizzie Lizzie, lovely mum; young Hillary, little Scouse lady; the charming Mrs Trace, and all the other stars of the X-ray department.

Such is the nature of the hospital, that it would be impossible not to accumulate many friends. The great bunch in CSSD, the eye department staff, with a special mention for Olive 'the champion char and coffee maker'; June, Sheila, Maureen and Sally in Quality Control; Mary and Phil on ITU, and all the domestic ladies. How could a hospital possibly function without its pathological laboratory? Having worked in this department, in a maintenance capacity of course, even I could understand its importance, not only to the hospital, but to the whole community. And last but not least, a section of the workforce that serves the whole of the hospital; the good old portering staff; vastly undervalued and vastly underpaid. Good days for me at QA Hospital. I wonder if this happy state of affairs will remain?

TIME FOR CELEBRATION

More good news for June and I; our dear daughter-in-law Sally had given birth to a darling little girl. We became proud grandparents on the 25th March 1985. I had always felt that somehow I had missed out by not having had a daughter. I do not mind one bit sharing our Mary. It is a wonderful feeling cradling your first child. The only feeling to equal this, is to cradle your first grandchild. Mary is fourteen years old now, and June and I are even more proud of her. People say it is better to be born lucky, more so than good looking. Let me tell you now, that I am certainly not good looking, but I am happy just to be lucky.

More good fortune was to smile on us as parents. Our second son David had been courting a charming young lady who had impressed June and I very much. This was Yvonne Hackney, and she lived in Copnor Road. Any parent will tell you that it is not any use whatsoever trying to push your child into marrying someone just because you just happen to like them. June and I did secretly hope that David and Yvonne would name the day, and to our great delight that is just what they did. Meeting Yvonne's parents was the pleasure that we both expected that it would be. Brenda and Maury were as easy to get along with as their daughter. As I have said, I always longed for a daughter, but when it comes down to arranging your daughter's wedding, I may have second thoughts. Not true of course, it made me very happy just to sit back and watch the happiness emanating from everyone, when discussing and making the arrangements for the big day. It seemed that in no time at all that the day for the wedding had arrived; a bitterly cold day; but who cared? The day was wonderful for everyone. Robert, the QA photographer, had kindly agreed to record the happy event, and many thanks to him for doing a fine job. I never had any doubts that he would!

ACCOUNTANTS V JOBS

A person would have to be a super optimist even to imagine that it would be possible to remain with one employer until retirement age. Realistically it is not a great deal to ask of a rich country, the basic right to be able to work and support your family. For the third time in my working life, rumours had begun regarding the future prospects of remaining in my present employment. Here was a situation almost identical to the experience that I had had with the demise of the Co-op building department; only this time good old privatization was to be the enemy.

Maybe it would be a good idea to give you a true picture of the happenings at this time. A part of my contract included working on outstations away from QA Hospital. A petrol allowance was made when using your own car. Also a meal allowance of three pounds, and five pounds for managers, when visiting your work site. Generally five people from QA did the work on the outstations. This was five too many according to the Trust's accountants. The fact was that this work would be put out to private contract, and five good tradesmen were to lose their jobs. We were given a list of contractors who had tendered for this work. One name on the list, was the name of a company who had their last contract terminated by hospital management because of seriously bad workmanship. This is a fact! The QA workforce were asked to complete the work, and also put right the shoddy work left behind by this company. You have already guessed, this cowboy outfit that were ordered off of the site, were the company to win this lucrative contract. In other words privatization at any cost! This lot were not alone in getting away with substandard work. I can remember full well having to clear up behind contractors working in Dunsbury Way Health Centre. Even as I write this, cleaning up behind subcontractors by NHS staff, is still going on in Queen Alexandra Hospital. "If five of you were to go now, it would help secure the jobs of the remainder." Now where have I heard that before? This was actually said by the hospital management.

By this time I had become really worried when considering my future, if any, working for the NHS. Of course, this situation had to be discussed with my dear wife. We had faced the very same situation only a few years before. After much discussion, we came to the conclusion that to avoid more worry it would be a good idea to work for myself. Reluctantly I took voluntary redundancy, seeing no future whatsoever at QA Hospital. As it happens, a lot of the tradesmen are still working in the building department, albeit under a different set-up, and I wish them all the luck in the world. Whatever would I do, not being able any more to have cups of tea with Pam, Pat and the other cleaning ladies on D level? As they say, all good things come to an end.

My wife and I were given the news that we could expect a new addition to our family. This time the news came from Yvonne and David. More happiness for both sets of parents, and of course more speculation; boy or a girl? The main consideration was 'Please come through the confinement safely'. It always gives parents a great deal of pleasure and satisfaction to observe your children caring for their children, and I will put on record that Sally and Yvonne have made a marvellous job of being mothers.

Another boy was born into the Franckeiss family. The name chosen for him was a name that the family have used for many years; from 1600 in fact. Yet another John Franckeiss; a darling little baby.

Earlier on in this story, I was bemoaning the fact that I had never had a daughter. Well, praise be, since the birth of John, Gary and Sally had decided to increase their family. Mary was to have a sister, Jessica. Yvonne decided that what one part of the family could do, she could do likewise, and to our great pleasure produce yet another girl; a little charmer named Kim.

Here I am the proud grandfather of four grandchildren; three of which are girls! What more could I ask of life? I am truly a lucky man.

My beloved grandchildren

Jessica   Mary

Kim   John

THE PASSING OF MY MOTHER, HOSPITAL FOR ME

The previous chapter ended with me crowing about how lucky I am. Please read on and be advised how fate can change the course of your life in seconds.

When my father passed away, my mother felt that she had no wish to continue living in the house at Leigh Park. With a little badgering of the housing officials, and the inevitable form filling, a fairly nice flat was found for her in Southsea. Once settled in her new home, and although she lived alone, she carried on in her independent way. She was always reluctant to ask for help, and would only do so when all else failed. Her words to me, said so many times were "You have your own lives to live and a family to care for. I have no wish to bother you unnecessarily." I knew that is how it had to be. My mother lived by her principles until the very end.

My brother Brian and his wife Lucy, had invited our mum to spend the weekend in their home in Chichester, with not a mention of the fact that she was feeling ill. She bid my brother and his wife good night and toddled off to bed. She passed away that night, probably in the way that she would have wanted, not the slightest bother to anyone.

My mother had experienced some hard times in her lifetime, but never did we hear never-ending recriminations. She had her family to care for, and that to her was all that mattered. A lovely lady, and I am proud to be her son.

Like all funerals, it was a very sad and sombre affair, but to make it even more sad, and to my utter disgust, three of my brothers deemed it unnecessary to pay their last respects. I hope that they all read this, and then come face to face with me and ask why I have written this fact into my story? That is easy to explain.

I am disgusted with the three of them!

My work had now taken me to Highlands Road in Emsworth to decorate the exterior of a house; a task that I had taken on and completed to the satisfaction of both myself and my customer very many times. Ladder work held no fears for me whatsoever. From the age of fourteen I had been working off of ladders with no apprehension whatever the height of the work. Maybe I had become blasé and careless in my use of ladders, which was to be the cause of my accident, just waiting to happen! Due to poor positioning of the ladder that I was using to reach guttering, and also an uneven surface, the ladder tilted and caused me to lose my balance and fall from seventeen feet onto a concrete driveway.

My injuries were serious, and I was taken to QA Hospital and admitted. After initial treatment in accident and emergency, an X-ray was arranged at once, and those lovely radiotherapy girls were more than a little surprised to see me in such dire circumstances, but at least I was a little more quieter than when I had often worked in their department. I was under sedation.

For a self-employed man to be hospitalised is very serious financially, and adds to the stress of having an accident and being unable to continue working. Having a mortgage and other commitments, as any working man will fully understand, a regular income is essential. Whilst lying in a hospital bed with ample time to mull things over, it tends to make one's mind work overtime. With the injuries that I had sustained, I firmly believed that it would be the end of my livelihood in the building trade. The next question being "How would I earn my living?" One brilliant ray of light that shone, in what was for me a very dark period, was the wonderful support that I had from my ex-colleagues of QA building department. Thank you lads for all chipping in to buy me an easy chair to use during my convalescence. Real friends indeed!!

WELL AT LEAST IT IS WORK

For the first time in my working life, I had to seek work from the Senior Employment Exchange, and for me it was the most degrading experience that I had ever had. To these people my accident was a non-event, or self-inflicted. No financial assistance whatsoever was forthcoming, solely because I was self-employed, and when I politely asked if it would help my case if I were a foreigner, I believe that I was near to being shot.

On the rare occasion that I was offered work, it would be of the short-term contract type, and more often than not in the region of two pounds an hour. This country had certainly gone backwards in many ways, certainly in terms of employment. This period in my life I will admit to being in a bit of depression, but I am fairly certain that when I say that periods like this will happen to most people.

This day as usual, I had been to the Labour Exchange, and sure enough, short-term and low pay work was all that was on offer. "If you don't show any interest, then we will stop your dole money." They even got that wrong, as I was not receiving any money at all. The jobs offered to me were too bad for me to even consider. Home again, and June and I were discussing the fact that we had begun to draw on our savings for day-to-day living, when the telephone interrupted our conversation. A dear lady by the name of Jill White, had rung to ask me if I would be interested in doing the job of a car parking attendant at QA and St Mary's Hospitals. My luck had changed. Of course I was interested. Car parking came under the jurisdiction of QA Building Department Small Works Management, of which Jill was the very competent secretary.

With my stay in hospital and period of convalescing, my time out of work amounted to eight months. Needless to say I was more than grateful for the offer of work, and I accepted the offer at once. Before I leave this section of the story regarding my accident, just let me say a heartfelt thanks to the staff of the hospital for taking care of me so well.

My work as a car parking attendant included servicing the pay machines; clearing the cash; renewing ticket rolls; be ready with change, for which I carried a float supplied by me; give directions; locate parking places at peak times (not easy) and generally help everyone as much as possible. Very often there would be a malfunction in the machines, and I was expected to locate and repair the fault. My orders were to use wheel clamps for parking offences, and I am very proud to say that I never resorted to this measure once during my time as a parking attendant.

My method of working was to help the staff as much as possible, which I did. I often turned a blind eye when observing staff parking where they had no right to park, also rooting-out members of staff who had left their lights on and informing them. I also used my skill of opening a locked door to regain ignition keys for some forgetful member of staff.

In general the staff and I got along very well, but as is always the case in any group of people, there will always be the oddballs. A male staff nurse, when politely asked to move his car, threatened to beat me to a pulp — charming! A consultant had parked his car in a space reserved for the disabled. All consultants had reserved parking facilities for their exclusive use, and it was something that I just had to check. When I approached the man, he threatened to give me a black eye. There was also the time when a member of the public, whom I had spotted using an out-of-date ticket, was asked by me to purchase a current ticket. This she did, but her husband paid me a visit later in the day 'to sort me out' as he so nicely put it.

Apart from the abuse that I had experienced, the event that decided me to move on, was the unfortunate event of a machine malfunctioning in QA car park whilst I was doing my duty in St Mary's Hospital. Panic stations! I had a mild telling off; unjustified I thought. It is difficult to understand how two engineers, with a combined salary of £40,000 or more, were unable to fix a machine that a lowly car parking attendant, on £5,000 per annum, could. Do you think this could be called riding on the backs of others?

To be able to earn a wage, it was my policy that being flexible was the most sensible approach, therefore when applications were invited for trainee care assistants at St James' Hospital, not believing that I would even be considered due to my track record as a building worker only, and also my age, I applied. My luck was still holding, and I was invited for an interview. My interview was a success, and in due course I was offered one of the vacancies, which I accepted. I have to say that the wages were very low, but at least it allowed my savings to remain intact, and my place of work would be within easy walking distance of my home.

Being a care assistant to people with psychiatric problems, is no easy task, and I did not expect it to be. However with training, listening and learning, and being guided along by the other care assistants and staff nurses, who were all wonderful; even Peter Jones!! I seemed to be making some progress in my new job.

As I have already stated, the work is very poorly paid and combined with a short-term contract, it did not make for a very satisfying situation, and added to this there was news of the unit being moved to Petersfield. By this time I had completed about seven months at St James' Hospital, and being on a wage of £82 per week, paying to travel to work and back, would have been out of the question. A short-term contract is just about what it says, every year a decision is made to either give you the sack or another year's work, and if you did not see eye-to-eye with a certain manager, then you were out. So once more I began to scan the internal vacancies' bulletin board for a position elsewhere in the Health Authority.

OUT OF THE FRYING PAN

A post had been advertised in-house for an assistant in the Sterile Supply Unit in St Mary's Hospital. It would mean another new challenge and complete change in my work. Without hesitation I applied for the post, and once more it would mean very low wages. This was no surprise, it was becoming the norm, and this work that I was expected to do was classified by the hospital as semi-skilled, so there could be very little argument. Once more I had been successful with my application, and I was asked to commence work as soon as possible.

Within a very short time of starting work at HSDU, I began to realise that the work that I was expected to do was way above the classification of semi-skilled; it was pure skill. Was classing the work as semi-skilled a subtle way of saying it only warranted a low wage? There would be no point in me trying to describe the many skilled processes of that department. What I will say is, without the many skills and know-how of these clever ladies who work in HSDU, the theatres and wards of St Mary's and QA Hospitals would cease to function.

Being elderly, it seems to me, tends to retard one's brain somewhat in learning new skills. My time in this department of St Mary's was never long enough to attain the skills of my colleagues, but what I lacked in skill I made up for in input. Dodging work has never been part of my working life. When I tell you that, at times in an eight-hour shift, it was necessary to have four changes of cotton shirt due to my perspiring, this is the absolute truth. Clearing and supplying eight operating theatres is a nonstop, very busy eight hours. Being a very conscientious type of person, I was always changed into sterile dress, and ready to start my shift, well before the official start time. There was no need, or pressure applied, for me to do this, it was just my way of doing things. If it was noticed, I do not know, and I certainly never gave it a second thought.

A certain lady supervisor was inclined to bullying. So far it had not affected me, but my turn was to come. I will say once more that those ladies were a lovely crowd to work with, and I suppose that it is inevitable that any one of those nice ladies could have been chosen as supervisor, but a rotten apple had got the job. Having completed my shift, and as usual made sure that everything was left in apple-pie order for the next member of a new shift, it was necessary to wash and rid myself of my work clothes. The handling of dozens of clinical waste bags, disposing of buckets of body fluids and many other distasteful items, gave me no wish to carry contamination into my own home. The time was 5.58 p.m.; two minutes before completion of shift. It was always my practice to go to the main work area to say cheerio to my colleagues. Unfortunately the shift supervisor thought that it was about time that she bullied someone. "You are not going, it is not yet six o'clock!" In a very quiet and restrained manner, I replied that in one minute's time it will be six o'clock. It had taken those few words to light the touch paper. From a female came these words, and I quote; "You will do as you are f****** well told, you do not f****** well go until I say so." That was the marvellous lady supervisor's way of talking to her charges. All this for two pounds an hour! I never gave this woman the satisfaction of hearing me answer her back. I walked away, and there and then decided to hand in my notice.

Had I taken the matter further, I am of the opinion that she would have been sacked. There was not much point in adding to her problems. In a strange sort of way, feeling sorry for her was the only option. The manager of the department and his assistant, I have no argument with, in fact I still consider them as two of my friends. Maybe I would have endured the bullying for a decent wage, but never for a pittance. Not a very satisfying end to a man's working life, but as they say, "There's nowt so queer as folk."

A DEDICATION

The last chapter was to have been the last, but a short while ago the tragic news of a relative's death was passed on to June and I; the death of Brett Carter, the much-loved son of Michelle and Nick, and the grandson of Anne and Sid Johns.

This dedication is to a very fine and courageous young man. From the age of eleven he had been suffering with, perhaps the most terrible disease of all, cancer. From that tender age he had entered a battle, but this horrible disease had a real adversary in this young man. Brett continued to do what any eleven-year-old would do, play his sports and take an interest in everyday things, although inwardly he must have been thinking what a chore it was to have to attend clinic or hospital for treatment, time after time. This is why I have found it necessary to tell you of this young man's battle to stay alive. Brett will not only be remembered for his fighting, as he was a gentle and thoughtful person. I heard this from a good source, his Nanny Babs, who had nothing but praise for her great-grandson. If there was an award for example and courage then surely it would be his. For four years he fought and yet remained his own unassuming self. Towards the end of the four years, he was given three months to live, and even pushed that three months into seven months. This disease never had it all its own way, Brett fought it, and in the fighting became exhausted. The odds were too great. This dear lad was to die in his sleep. He was nearly fifteen years old.

My condolences go out to the whole family, especially to Nick and Michelle, who stood their ordeal with great dignity. They will miss this fine son so much, but they can take heart in the fact that they did their utmost to ease his pain and suffering.

CONCLUSION

There is very little left for me to say, except perhaps if I can be as fortunate in the remainder of my life, as I have been for the sixty-six years that I have lived thus far, then I will never have cause to complain.

Thank you for reading this story of my life. I realise that a big percentage has been taken up with describing my working experiences, and I make no apologies for this. It is the story of a working man and his endeavours to provide for his family in the only way possible, working with his hands.

When I die my family will not inherit a fortune, but in this story I have tried to convey my feelings and love for all of them; finding it easier to put into words than by demonstration. Of course, this story is not only about me. It takes two people to make a family, and I can give thanks for my great fortune in finding a wife like my dear June. A gentle and kind person, a wonderful mother, dearly loved by her children and grandchildren.

May I conclude with a wish? That the good fortune that has smiled on me in my lifetime will smile on all of the readers of this story.

THE END